MW00464098

"Troy Vines has written a[n] absolute wonders of the h[uman] by his medical training, not only highlight the intricate design that demands a designer, but also the mysteries of the body that are inexplicable apart from God. It turns out Troy is not only an outstanding doctor, but an astute observer of God's creative and sustaining work in all of us. This is an excellent read for doubters and believers alike. I highly recommend this book!"

DR. JIMMY ADCOX, Discipleship Minister and Former
Senior Minister, Southwest Church, Jonesboro, AR

"Dr. Vines is obviously skilled in medicine but his own fascination with the creator is evident and inviting throughout the book. Nonscientific readers will appreciate the clear descriptions of how parts of the body work and those searching for God will certainly find him here. Chapters such as "The Eye" brought me greater understanding to the miraculous complexity of God's design in sight yet reminded me that God designed it to encounter him. Dr. Vines connects the concepts of medicine and belief with ease and engages the reader like a good doctor, but the kind of doctor that we all really want, one who is a trusted mentor and wise friend in the journey to discover God."

JENNIFER BARNETT, Executive Director of
Freedom Prayer, Author of *First Freedoms* and
Co-author of *Freedom Tools*, Nashville, TN

"This book is a must read for anyone on a journey of faith. Where science and faith are often pitted against one another, Dr. Vines masterfully weaves the two together from his own life experiences. Expect to be inspired, encouraged and better equipped to answer life's big question about the origin of life."

TRAVIS EADES, Lead Minister, Oak
Hills Church, San Antonio, TX

"Dr. Vines has written a tremendous book that melds the intricacies of the human body with a living, vibrant faith in God. By working readers through the complexity and beauty of the human body, Dr. Vines invites us to consider God's artistry anew. As readers consider this work, they are encouraged to process Scripture and thought-provoking questions related to each of the seven wonders of the human body. The book is an excellent resource for those seeking clarification on the grand design of humanity."

CHRIS HARRELL, Senior Minister,
Compass Church, Jonesboro, AR

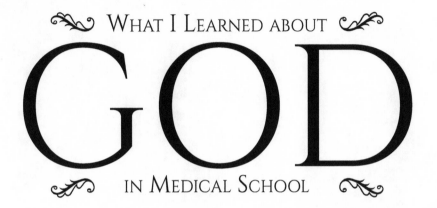

WHAT I LEARNED ABOUT

GOD

IN MEDICAL SCHOOL

TROY VINES, M.D.

ISBN 978-1-68570-029-4 (paperback)
ISBN 978-1-68570-030-0 (digital)

Copyright © 2021 by Troy Vines, M.D.

All rights reserved. No part of this publication may be reproduced, distributed, or transmitted in any form or by any means, including photocopying, recording, or other electronic or mechanical methods without the prior written permission of the publisher. For permission requests, solicit the publisher via the address below.

Christian Faith Publishing
832 Park Avenue
Meadville, PA 16335
www.christianfaithpublishing.com

Printed in the United States of America

CONTENTS

NOT WHAT I EXPECTED

Apologetics is a word that refers to the branch of theology devoted to the defense of the divine origin and authority of Christianity. There are many excellent books on the subject in which authors have devoted hours upon hours of research in an attempt to provide proof of God's existence and our divine origin. Data from geological conclusions, recordings from eyewitnesses at the time of Jesus, biblical storylines that were corroborated by non-Christian writers, failed attempts to create life in the lab, and many more examples have been included in that research. There are also books and research in support of a nontheological origin to humanity. To be honest, there are intelligent people with PhD at the end of their names that battle on each side of the issue of human origin and whether or not God even exists.

Albert Einstein said, "Science without religion is lame; religion without science is blind." After having gone through the academics to become a physician, I agree. Because of the desire on both sides to have an either/or mentality, we have missed out on some of the important aspects of both science and religion that can lead to an enriched life. Some nonbelievers agree that there is design to the human body but no designer. Then the question must be, who or what provides the design? Then there are those believers who agree that God is our creator without giving much thought to the use of scientific evidences to more completely understand the human being. While I don't expect to resolve the issues that may have developed on each side, I do hope that you will follow along in the book and come to an understanding that both parties can coexist to provide a more complete understanding of the physical, mental, and spiritual aspects of the human being.

As I entered medical school, I did not expect to exit the other side of my studies with a greater faith in God. It was through medical school and understanding the science of the human body that I was led to an unwavering truth that a creator does exist—and not only that he exists but that he is the creator of our majestic body and how it functions. Because of these truths that I learned in medical school, it subsequently led me on a journey to find a more complete answer to explain certain functions that occur within the human body that were not covered in those medical classes—not just to understand *how* the body functions but also to understand *what* makes certain parts of the body react in the ways that they react. In doing so, I discovered a newfound understanding of how a component that dwells within each of us can lead us to a healthier existence here on earth. It is a component that is interactive with our Creator. It will be discussed more in-depth in chapter 8 and the conclusion of the book.

Rather than presenting hours upon hours of research, I want this book to be about you, the reader, doing the research simply as you go through your daily routine. Hopefully, it will be so simple that you will not feel that you have done research at all. By that, I mean that I will give you key information about the human body to consider as you go through your week-to-week journey in life. You will see, hear, touch, smell, and taste the evidence daily. I hope this will help you develop your own thoughts about the question of the existence of God and our creation. Someone has said, "Truth is discovered, not invented." Gravity was discovered by Newton but was not invented by him. Absolute truth occurs when there is no other possibility for why something works or occurs. My guess is that if you approach this book with an open mind, the drawn conclusion at the end will be an absolute affirmation of God and the divine origin of the human species.

While I want to look at the "seen things" around us to make a case for God's existence, I will discuss one "unseen thing" within each human being that I believe is important for the function of many human organs—one that will explain the unexplainable aspects of *what* makes certain organs function the way that they do within the body, one that was not discussed in medical school because science alone does not have the answer as to *why* some organs behave as they do. It is a component that is interactive with the brain and even present in the function of other organs. It is one, in my opinion, that could help you achieve not only a physically, mentally, and emotionally healthier life but could enrich your life with peace and joy that you probably thought was beyond your reach.

CHAPTER 1

THE DECISION

It has been estimated that we make thousands of decisions each day.[1] Some decisions have greater future consequences than do other decisions. The consequences of some decisions may affect us for an hour or a day while others may affect us for a lifetime. Some of the major decisions may include who to date, what career to choose, where to live, and whether to have children.

There is one decision that is likely made by everyone at some stage of life: Should I or should I not believe in a higher being that created me and the world around me? Like many other decisions, multiple additional decisions may follow, depending on the answer to that one. For instance, if I believe in a higher being, who or what is the higher being, and what do I do next? Or if I don't believe in a higher being, where did I come from, and what is my future? What are the evidences that support either decision? What role does science play? How do science and biblical theology coexist, or can they?

There are some obvious implications attached to whether or not I believe in a higher being or God. When speaking of the existence of God, C. S. Lewis stated,

> Christianity, if false, is of no importance,
> and if true, of infinite importance. The only
> thing it cannot be is moderately important.

If we decide that God does not exist, then we continue in a world where our day-to-day choices in life, in the end, can only give us a conscious certainty of death without hope.[2] If, however, we arrive at the decision that God does exist and that he created us and the world around us, we should be intensely interested in his guidance and his purpose for our lives. This intense interest is not just to attain the final end goal of experiencing a new heaven coming down to earth[3] when this life is over. That guidance is to help us daily, as well as during critical times in our lives, to experience freedom, joy, and peace that can only be found in a creator who wrote the human owner's manual—a manual that is from a God who is not of but is in this world. Belief in God's existence and that he is the creator of the universe is the cornerstone for developing faith and trust in God. Our developed faith and trust in God can then lead us to an unbelievable life that only few choose to experience in its fullness while living on this earth.

My Story

I grew up in a small faith-based town with a population of 450. Like most children, my faith as a child consisted of the faith of my parents. During my preteen years, we would attend church services infrequently. I received some amount of Bible knowledge and was introduced to the larger-than-life faith-based stories of Adam and Eve, Noah, Moses, Joseph, Samson, David and Goliath, and of course, Jesus. Within these stories came the interactions that God had with each individual.

As I became a teen, I experienced a gnawing internal sense that God existed—not only existed but that I was drawn to him in a way that I had not felt before. As I worked through this period of time, I thought this stronger belief in God's existence might be a primal reaction in response to preachers pointing to the woes of those who did not believe God. (We had a few preachers who could really "bring it" as it related to sermons on the topic of hell.) But within the content of the Bible and the context of the preacher's sermons, there seemed to be something greater than just a response to fear. So at the age of sixteen, I responded to God's call and confessed to becoming a disciple and was baptized.

During the next couple of years, my faith seemed fairly stable with a few exceptions of wandering for brief periods. Then in my late teen and early adult years, my belief and trust seemed to waver. I still declared myself a Christian, taught Bible classes, and contributed to my church family in various ways. However, somewhere in the deep, dark recesses of my mind, I was asking myself, "Am I just spinning my wheels in a universe that is running itself? Maybe God doesn't exist." I was also perplexed at that time because of some difficult life situations that had occurred to some of my friends who seemed to be following God.

Despite all this, I could not find another plausible explanation for our existence that really made sense. I believed in evolution occurring within a species to some degree but did not believe there was enough evidence for one species to pole vault in development and become another species. I did not believe that Darwinian evolution, as I knew it, could explain creation of humanity and the other creations in our midst.

I was left with several questions: If God exists, how do we know? What are the evidences of his existence? How real are these evidences? How can we see God without physically seeing him?

We love to be able to use our senses to see, hear, smell, taste, and touch something before we want to declare it real. Are there any evidences currently available that would satisfy our senses without the physical aspect of actually seeing, hearing, and touching God or Jesus?

Can we know *for sure* that God exists? Not many things in life are known with 100 percent assurance. Is God's existence one of those? Are there evidences that speak to us that totally convince us that God exists beyond a doubt? Is there "confidence in what we hope for and assurance about what we do not see?"[4] Someone has said that the only two things in life that are sure are death and taxes. Recently, with tax cyber theft, even some aspects of taxes are not a surety. So how was I to answer all the questions that were running through my mind?

Medical School

The answer for me began at age 26. My educational background included taking prepharmacy credits at Arkansas State University and then attending pharmacy school at the University of Arkansas Medical Center School of Pharmacy. I received my undergraduate degree in pharmacy at age 21 and worked at pharmacies owned by other pharmacists until age 26. At that time, I decided to establish my own pharmacy, enter into hospital pharmacy, where more acquired knowledge in pharmacy could be utilized, or apply to medical school to obtain an MD degree. I applied to the University of Arkansas School of Medicine and was accepted.

What transpired during the next four years is what increased my faith in God, began a transformation in my life, and is the subject of this book. As the study of all the aspects of the human body unfolded, it answered the questions as to the existence of God that I had posed earlier in this chapter. The intricate detail in which we are made left no doubt in my mind that we were created by a higher being. The evidences were multiple and compelling. They were real and could be evaluated by multiple senses. I was able to "see" God without physically touching him.

Throughout the remainder of this book, I will describe in some detail the different organs or organ systems that compose the body. I will emphasize areas that for me were the most convincing in my journey as I established a belief in the existence and sovereignty of God as the only answer for such a complex body to exist and function. I will describe several of the major functions of each body part or organ system and how they interconnect to form our brilliantly created body. I will only scratch the surface of the information that technology has made available about the organs themselves and the chemical reactions that occur within them. I will discuss how the body's function is dependent on these chemical reactions to occur in certain sequences. If only a minor change occurs within these sequences, we often cease to exist. Multiple times, I will pose the questions to you, the reader: "Is this something that required divine intervention, *or* is this something that just happened by chance?" You decide.

As I mentioned in the introduction, I want this book to be about you, the reader. In chapters 3 through 9, I will give you several key thoughts about a component of the human body. I hope you will spend a week on that chapter leisurely thinking about that component's importance to life, the sophistication of the component, the interaction of the component with other organs or chemicals, and the likelihood of it requiring divine design.

Before we look at these incredible organs and organ systems and how they work, in the next chapter, I want us to explore a biblical text in Romans. Regardless of whether or not you believe in the Bible or that the writers were inspired, the content of this text will allow for an independent analysis of things that are visible before you. I think this text is key to how we approach the development of our decision on the existence of God. I also want to briefly discuss a theory that is opposed to the biblical presentation of God's creation of the human being and why I think that the theory is flawed. Then I will touch on how technology has overwhelmingly strengthened the case for God's existence. Then I will introduce thoughts about what makes different organs continue to function despite the fact that they are not receiving any input generated by the human body. As I unfold the facts that lead to the truth of God's existence, my hope is that it will become more apparent why we should be intensely interested in his guidance and purpose for our lives.

CHAPTER 2

GOD IS CLEARLY SEEN

For since the creation of the world, *God's invisible qualities*—his eternal power and divine nature—have been *clearly seen*, being understood by *what was made*, so that people are *without excuse*.[5]

—Romans 1:20 (emphasis added)

There are times when we read a sentence or a thought in a book and do not grasp the full meaning. Perhaps it is because we are thinking about dinner, rushing through the material because of time restraints, or just in a phase of life when the statement does not seem important. This statement in Romans 1:20 was made by Paul, a follower of Jesus and writer in the New Testament. It was not until I began to look closer at the design of the human body that his statement took on a deeper meaning. Paul's statement is unique in that whether or not you believe that Paul was a writer inspired by the Holy Spirit, his challenge about how to prove God's existence is based on our independent analysis of the things around us. Also, his statement does not require one to believe in the existence of God as a prerequisite. All that is really required is an open mind along with the senses of sight, touch, smell, taste, and hearing that already exists within us. These senses are then used to evaluate "the things that have been made."

When we evaluate the created things around us, several thoughts come to mind. First, it does not require you to be a person of high intelligence for you to do the evaluation. There may be some who have the ability to examine at a deeper level than others, but for the most part, everyone has the ability to decide whether or not it requires a higher being to create the things around us. It does not require a Harvard degree in order to engage our senses and evaluate what is before us. In fact, sometimes that can be a detriment especially if one has already been convinced that science, by itself, holds the key to explaining every aspect of what is seen.

Second, we have been gifted the senses of sight, hearing, smell, touch, and taste in order to assess what has been made. It is easy for each of us to use the sense of sight to see the beauty in nature. A sunset, a rainbow, the colors found in a peacock, or snow on a mountaintop are just a few. We use our sense of smell to enjoy the fragrance of a flower or to decide to turn away from the pungent odor of a skunk. We use our sense of hearing to listen to our family member discuss his or her day or to be warned of an approaching train. We use our sense of taste to enjoy our favorite prepared food. One of the more important of the senses is touch. Without it, babies would not develop correctly emotionally. Touch is our primary language of compassion. We will discuss the intricacy of these senses as we go forward in the study of the body.

Third, we don't have to drive a hundred miles in order to see God's creative power at work. We don't even have to walk off our property to see the stars, smell the flowers, touch our pet, hear an owl at a distance, or experience a function within the human body. God's creative powers have produced a plethora of items all around each one of us regardless of where we live or what we do on a daily basis.

Finally, for a full evaluation to occur, at any level, seeing what is made can only be achieved by processing the information with an open mind. Being open to allow our brain to process these items and fully access everything that we see is important.

As you evaluate these created things around us, I hope you will see that a large amount of eternal creativity and divine power have gone into them. As we move forward, I will attempt to show that the creative nature and eternal power within the creation of the human body, though very complex, are easily seen and understood.

Darwin's Theory

My approach to providing information to allow you to look fully at the miracle known as the human body, in order to let you decide about a divine creator, is independent of thoughts for or against a theory known as Darwin's theory. I believe you will clearly see that the interactive intricacies of the human body are enough to reveal that a creator was and still is present.

There are those who believe and espouse that the human body arose from simpler forms of life, even from a single cell. Most who believe this are students of a man's work that became known as Darwin's theory. But where does Darwin's theory even fit into the discussion of God's existence and divine origin of the human body? I would like to offer a few thoughts about his theory.

This theory is based on a large body of work done by Charles Darwin as logged in his book *The Origin of Species* published in 1859. Darwin's arguments advanced his theory of natural selection and seemed to counter the idea that the human (and other) species were not created in whole by a divine creator but started with simpler forms that mutated along the way to produce a fully functional life. At the time, his book, which took twenty years to compile, was read and believed by many scientists as a possible alternative to the divine creation of man and other species.

The first question we must ask is, "What is a theory"? It is "a proposed explanation whose status is still conjectural and subject to experimentation, in contrast to well-established propositions that are regarded as reporting matters of actual fact."[6] Darwin's theory, while interesting at the time of his writing, was hampered during his lifetime by a lack of technology that many years later became commonplace. Advances in microscopes, CAT scans, electron microscopy, and other investigative tools have revealed complexities that were undiscoverable during Darwin's time. These more recent revelations of the human body have made Darwin's theoretical works educated guesses for his time. He was projecting thought based on gross anatomy but did not have the evidence currently available through technology to fully see the intricate, amazing functions of our cells, organs, and the biochemistry interactions that occur to realize the entirety of the human. After the information from these technological advances surfaced, a large part of the scientific community disengaged from Darwin's theory.

In 1996, Michael J. Behe wrote a very compelling book entitled *Darwin's Black Box* which is highly recommended if you want to critically look at more evidence for intelligent design in our creation. In the preface of his book, Behe makes the statement that

> It was once expected that the basis of life would be exceedingly simple...but the elegance and complexity of biological systems at the molecular level have paralyzed science's attempt to account for the origin of specific, complex biomolecular systems, much less any progress... there are compelling reasons—based on the structure of the systems themselves—to think that a Darwinian explanation for the mechanisms of life will forever prove elusive.[7]

His book goes on to offer proof for his thoughts.

Not only was Darwin unable to see within the human cell (one of his "black boxes") to view the components of each cell, he was unable to reveal all the many functions that the cell produced in order to make human life possible as well as functional.

Most of us have heard of the term *chemical reaction*. It is a process in which one or more chemical reactants come together and are converted into one or more different products. A biochemical reaction is simply a chemical reaction that occurs within a living cell. One of the eleven functions that occurs within each cell (and there are trillions of cells) in our body is the breakdown of food molecules with a release of energy. This is known as cellular respiration. This function requires a complex biochemical event which is cyclical, whereby the cell is primed to release this stored energy. These cyclical reactions, known in biochemistry as the Kreb's cycle, require eight chemical reactions in order to produce ATP (adenosine triphosphate) and resultant energy. (See Diagram 1.)

I will let you examine a good biochemistry book to find out exactly how each step in the cycle works. After you do that, you will see why I did not go into an explanation of that in this book. I still get a little nervous just thinking about having to memorize the steps in the Kreb's cycle in our biochemistry class in medical school. However, this cycle is central to many other human body reactions that help to produce end products such as amino acids, cholesterol, and products required to form DNA and RNA. The exact replication of this and other biochemical processes occurs within trillions of cells many times a day. The chances of this happening while producing the same products over and over would be zero if attempting to understand it purely on a scientific basis. However, it continues to happen daily, over and over in every human being.

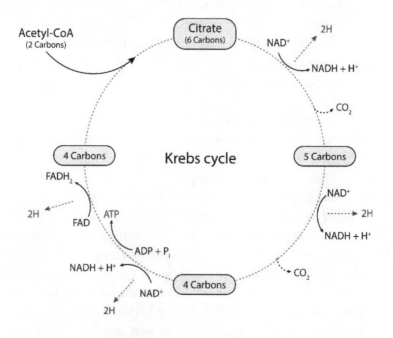

Diagram 1: The Kreb's Cycle

I think you can start to see just how limited Darwin was in his ability to understand the human body. I also think you can start to see how these biochemical reactions occurring over and over on a daily basis in such a precise way could not happen by chance.

It's Time to Go In

Seldom do we stop to think about the amazing functions of the human body and how they interconnect. For the most part, we take it for granted until a biochemical reaction or an organ fails to perform in the exact way expected, and we develop symptoms that are perceived. Prior to medical school, I had learned in pharmacy school how medications were dispersed, absorbed, transported to the intended sites in the body where they worked, what drugs they interacted with, and how the residual material of the drug was transported out of the body in addition to other information. In pharmacy school, it was more about the complexity of how the medications were made and the steps that were involved in order for the drug to be effective. It was not until engaging in medical school that I started to think about the complexity of the anatomy of the body, the interactions of the organ systems, how the body reacted to insults, and the wide range of biochemical reactions that take place minute by minute and sometimes second by second—reactions that could result in death if disturbed by an internal or external insult to one of these biochemical processes.

I applied to the University of Arkansas School of Medicine and was accepted. Sometime that fall, I was standing, along with approximately 130 of my classmates, in a hallway of one of the upper floors of the UAMS medical center. The double doors of a large room opened, and a voice rang out that echoed down the hall—"It's time to go in." It was time to expose ourselves to the gross anatomy lab. This was to be one of our first opportunities to really discover the human body. We were to spend the next three to four months dissecting the bodies beginning with the skin and ending with the evaluation of the deep internal organs.

For many of us, it was the first time to even touch a dead human body, let alone do a scalpel dissection of one. You could tell that there was a degree of anxiety within most of us as we did not know for sure how we would react to the task at hand. Our anxiety was exemplified by how quietly we all entered the room. I am sure that several of us experienced dry mouths, increased heartrates, and overactive sweat glands. As we entered, our senses of touch, smell, and sight were engaged. In the room, we saw thirty-four tables each with a cadaver (a dead body, especially for the purpose of being dissected) that was covered by a sheet. Our professor made sure that we knew that we were to respect each of the cadavers.

He stated, "Some of the cadavers that you are responsible for have lived lives of prestige and donated their bodies to science. Some were homeless. Some died from an illness, and attempts to find family failed. Each one deserves our utmost respect."

Each table would have four or five students surrounding it. Those four or five students would methodically dissect through the cadaver to locate all the nerves, blood vessels, organs, and other parts of the body that were required of us to visualize and learn. Also engaged was the sense of smell. The high-grade oil that was used as a preservative for the bodies had a unique odor. Even with removing and leaving our dissection coats in the anatomy lab, we could still smell the odor of the oil on our person. There was some truth to the statement that "you could always tell who a freshman medical student was by how they smelled."

As that semester progressed, all of us were able to see, as expected, that the nerves, blood vessels, organs, bones, and ligaments all followed the exact pattern of locality and structure. In this respect, God has made all of us the same. Except for the differences of male and female organs, whether the skin of the cadaver was white, black, brown, or other skin tone, whether they were of Spanish, African, English, Oriental or some other descent, this pattern of locality and structure held true. Everyone in the room knew those facts going into the gross anatomy course, but it was different experiencing that for ourselves as we were being fascinated by how the body was put together in a way that one part supported or aided another part. But the fascination was just getting started.

Over the next four years, the volume of information that we were asked to review and learn about the human body was significant. At that time, it was said that for every ten succeeding years, the amount of information about the human body doubled. With more recent technology, I am sure that that time interval has decreased. Tens of thousands of books have been written about the structure, function, and biochemical reactions of the body.

My goal in the next eight chapters of this book is not to try to expound or focus of how complex the human body is. In fact, I want to proceed in the other direction. I hope that you will be able to see how God made our very complex body function in such a simple but amazing way that we all can understand. It is through this process of looking at that dichotomy of complexity and simplicity that we can come to understand that God is *clearly seen* by one of the things he has made—the human body. There are many, many other mammals, birds, plants, insects, and natural landmarks that reveal the beauty and nature of God. Things such as the caterpillar converting to a butterfly, the peacock, the eagle soaring high in the sky, Niagara Falls, or the beauty of a sunset are all items in which God is clearly seen as well.

I will only be revealing the human body for your consideration as one of the many created things that God has revealed. Some of the information in each chapter may encourage you to examine other things that God has created. If that happens, I would consider that a bonus. I hope to present the next eight chapters in a way that is accurate, fun, and inspiring but requires very little time out of your day in order to process your thoughts. I believe that the truth found in the statement in Romans 1:20 was placed there so that *everyone* would be able to see and experience God, whether educated at an elite college or with little or no educational background at all. I also believe that sensing God's existence, seeing our origin as that from a divine creator, learning ways to interact with that Creator, and seeing that there is reason to be interested in God, are all things that you can affirm as you work through this book. I believe that God has given us these evidences. If we fail to see them, we are *without excuse*. So hang on for the ride. This is not going to be what you expected either.

The Seven Wonders of the Human Body

In school, you may have learned the Seven Wonders of the Ancient World. The Pyramid of Giza, the Hanging Gardens of Babylon, and the Colossus of Rhodes are three of those. They were known as wondrous feats of mankind. They did not, however, defy explanation. Before I get to the seven organs and organ systems that we are to discuss, I want you to consider what I will call "The Seven Wonders of the Human Body." I will discuss one of these in each chapter as we look at the remainder of the book (along with multiple other wonders of each organ or organ system). Here is my list of the top seven wonders of the human body. These seven wonders are within organs or organ systems that are seen with the human eye and, except for a creator's touch, defy explanation. There is one wonder that I consider greater that these seven. That wonder cannot be seen with the human eye. We will discuss it in chapter 8 as it relates to the brain and then unfold this wonder more completely in the conclusion.

Seven wonders of the human body—these wonders continue to amaze me to this day:

- The eye's formation of images
- The heart's indwelling pacemaker
- The lung's oxygen-carbon dioxide exchange
- The skin's process of wound healing
- The GI system's breakdown and conversion of food into energy
- The brain's formation of thoughts and ideas
- Pregnancy and formation of new life

Chapter 3

The Eye

Four facts about the eye:

1. The eye functions like a camera. The image you actually see is formed within your brain.
2. Each eye has six attached muscles that allow you to move the eye in all directions.
3. The eye has over one hundred million light-sensitive cells called rods and cones.
4. The eye cannot be transplanted due to millions of nerves within the optic nerve that connects it to the brain.

In this and each of the following six chapters, I will attempt to describe a different organ or organ system in the human body. Your first task, as the reader, is to evaluate the structures, features, and functions of that organ or organ system independent of what you have read, seen, or heard prior to now. Consider the complexity of its function. Also consider the consistency of its positioning from one human to another. Next, consider how the organ or organ system interrelates with the other organs or tissues of the body in order to provide a body function such as image formation or body movement. The next task is for you to answer the question, "Is this something that just developed by chance, *or* is this something that required divine intervention?"

I have decided to start with the eye. This very small organ is not critical to sustain life like the heart or lungs. However, it is, in my opinion, the organ that best represents the different layers of complexity that exists within it. (Except for the brain, I consider the eye to be the next most complex organ.)

For those of us fortunate enough to experience sight, it is often the first sense that is aroused upon awaking each morning. Without forethought, we open our eyelids, and if the light is good, a color image automatically appears. We don't stop to think about how that image develops so quickly and so accurately. If our eyes are healthy, the image allows us to reach out and grab a tissue or see how to get into our house shoes; or when we get out of bed and turn to go out of the room, the image stays in focus despite us turning our head. How is it that we can see to our right, to our left, up, down, and all the angles in between without moving our head, and the image stays clear?

Many other amazing functions of our eyes are occurring multiple times a day without conscious thought. For instance, what happens within the eye that allows it to quickly adjust to be able to see silhouettes when a light is turned off in a dark room? Why do our eyes tear when we are sad? If we have two eyes, why do we see only one image? What happens to the eyes that require us to need glasses? What happens that causes our vision to change drastically when only minor changes develop in and around the eye?

The eye is one of the many organs in the body that requires more than just the eye itself to complete its bodily function. Some have labeled this as an irreducibly complex system.

Wikipedia defines *irreducible complexity* as

> the argument that certain biological systems cannot have evolved by successive small modification to preexisting functional systems through natural selection because no less complex system would work.

26

In other words, for the eyes to function and maintain the image in the different settings that I just described, it requires the brain to receive and form an image through the optic nerve, muscles to move the eyes, tear ducts to provide tears, and multiple biochemical reactions to occur precisely and in sequence. If any of these inter-acting parts do not develop into their component, or if one step in the irreducibly complex process does not take place to complete the basic functions of that step, then the image is distorted or not pro-duced at all. For the eye to have evolved as some Darwinists suggest, there would have had to be many—and I mean incalculable—lucky mutations that occurred not only in the eye but also in the brain, eye muscles, and at the biochemical level. Not only would these muta-tions have had to occur, they would have had to develop at precisely the same time, or in rapid sequence, for vision to have taken place.

Let's look at the structure, features, and functions of the eye and the supporting organs and biochemical processes that we have learned through science. As we do this for the eye and the other organs and organ systems in the upcoming chapters, remember the quote of Albert Einstein in the introduction section of this book. He said, "Science without religion is lame; religion without science is blind." Medical school was the vehicle in which I learned the science pertaining to the human body that led me to a conclusion of proof of God's existence and of the absolute necessity of divine creation.

Through the use of technology such as the CAT scan, the elec-tron microscope, and other technological devices that were not avail-able during Darwin's time, science has uncovered the structure of the human eye. (See Image 1.)

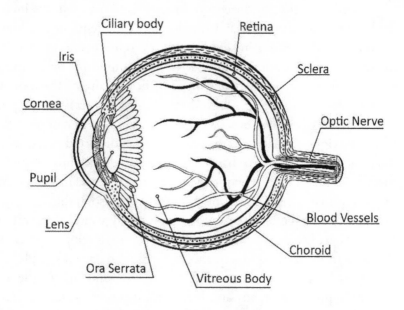

Image 1: The Human Eye

This diagram reveals the major structural components of the eye. Some of the functions and biochemical reactions will be explained as we discuss the structural components. Understanding the structure of the eye is necessary to understand what occurs in our routine daily activities that produces these amazing images.

The cornea acts as an outer lens in the eye. It functions to control and focus light entry into the eye. It produces about 70 percent of the total focus for the eye. When light hits the cornea, it is bent or refracted onto the lens of the eye. The cornea is the very sensitive part of the outer eye that tells us when something lands on the eye that could cause irritation or damage. Perhaps the most amazing aspect of the cornea is that unlike almost every other part of the body, it has no blood vessels and, therefore, no color. This allows for image clarity and initial refractory ability before light enters the lens. Scientists have recently discovered the reason that the cornea does not produce blood vessels. It is because of the production of a protein that inhibits growth factors which are the driving force for blood vessel formation.

The lens, along with the cornea, focuses the light coming into the eye onto the retina. Actually, our eyes see everything upside down. As light is refracted through a convex lens, it causes the information to be flipped. When we are looking at something, the image goes through the convex eye lens, and by the time it hits the retina, it is inverted, or upside down. This upside-down information is sent to the brain, which converts that data and turns it into a right-side-up image. Imagine trying to walk around if everything seemed to be upside down.

The lens can change its shape, which causes the eye's focal distance to change. It does this to create a clear image of what is being seen. For a clear image, the lens must also be clear. A cataract is a condition in which the lens is cloudy, hence producing a cloudy image. Removal of the lens (cataract) followed by replacement of the lens with an artificial lens can again produce a clear image.

The cells in the retina absorb and convert the focused light into electrochemical impulses that are transferred along the optic nerve. The retina receives light in the more than one million light-sensing rods and cones that are found within the retina. The rods tend to function better in dim light and give the black-and-white vision (hence the perception of silhouettes in dim light) while the cones function in brighter light and help with the perception of color. There are 120 million rod cells and approximately 6 to 7 million cone cells.

The optic nerve receives these impulses from the retina and transmits all the light information including brightness, color, and contrast. It conducts these impulses and is responsible for two very important neurological reflexes. One is the light reflex. This reflex is responsible for the constriction of both pupils when light is introduced into either eye. The other is the accommodation reflex. This reflex refers to the thickening of the lens when one looks at near objects such as when you read. Both of these changes have to occur in order that the image received and produced by the brain is clear. The optic nerve fibers carry information to the visual cortex of the brain found in the occipital (back) lobe of the brain. This part of the brain tells us what we are seeing.

There are twelve cranial (those related to the skull or head) nerves. The optic nerve is the second. (CNII.) As an examiner views the optic nerve with an ophthalmoscope, they are actually looking at an extension of the brain tissue. This is the only internal human tissue of its type that can be directly seen by the human eye with the aid of a medical apparatus. All other tissues of that type require the use of an imaging study such as a CAT scan or MRI.

Some of the receptors and chemical ingredients to make the rods and cones as well as the optic nerve transmit the visual signal include cyclic guanosine 3'–5' monophosphate (cGMP), transducin G protein-coupled receptor, and a derivative of vitamin A called retinal. Many other transmitting chemicals and protein changes occur in order to get the visual image from the cornea to the occipital area of the brain. (Most people, other that biochemists, tend to get a little bored discussing these chemicals and their reactions. I just wanted to mention a few in order to get a sense of the complexity of all the components that occur in order to fuel the events producing a visual image. If interested in further reactions, refer to a good biochemistry textbook on the biochemical reactions within the eye/brain.)

In addition to the structural components of the eye that have been mentioned, each eye has six attached muscles. These muscles aid in moving the eye in all directions, which decreases the need to move the head. There are four muscles (superior rectus, inferior rectus, medial rectus, and lateral rectus) that move the eye up, down, to the right, and to the left. The other two muscles (superior oblique and inferior oblique) help in moving the eye inward toward the nose and upward when the eye is looking in toward the nose. Each of these muscles have more than the simple singular function that I listed. This allows the eye to move smoothly while looking at the border of a rounded object and still maintain a clear image.

Another accessory of the eye is the tear gland, also known as the lacrimal gland. It is located above and toward the outside part of the eye. The tear glands produce a pH or acid-neutral liquid that helps to provide eye lubrication, clear debris or irritants, and helps aid the immune system by washing out organisms that could infect the eye. Then there is the tear duct that is located beside the upper nose which drains excess tears away from the eye and into the nose. That is why your nose may become moist and drain when you cry.

In addition to the connection that the eye has with the brain through the optic nerve, the images that the eye projects and the brain produces has an effect on our mental health. I was a small part of a medical mission team in 1989 that was led by Partners in Progress, who traveled to Guyana, South America. The people we visited in Guyana had little access to medical care. We divided into medical teams consisting of a physician, dentist, nurse, pharmacy tech, and an optometry assistant. After forming teams, each team would travel to our individual sites. We had collected medications via pharmaceutical samples. We had received eyeglasses from people who either had a change in their eyeglass prescription or had an extra pair. The physicians helped mostly with general health education and diagnosing things like hypertension. We were able to help with a couple of life-threatening illnesses while we were there.

I remember one child with meningitis while we were there. Had she not been treated, that child would have most certainly died. The dentist pulled several teeth that were causing pain and other health issues. They also provided education for good oral care that could prevent life-threatening illnesses. The nurses and pharmacy techs were very helpful with education and medication assistance. However, the people on our team who made the greatest impact in the lives of the people at their visits, and most likely long term, were the optometry assistants. Many of the people that we treated in Guyana were older. Glasses, for most, were either not available or were not affordable. One of my greatest joys during that trip was to take a break from what I was doing to watch the optometry assistants fit the people of Guyana for glasses. The broad smiles that ran across their faces as they slipped on a pair of glasses were priceless. They could actually read again, see their children clearly, and not trip over things. In addition to the smiles, there was jubilation with some of them as they danced around because of this newfound renewal of their sight. It was amazing that none of them complained about the shape or color of their frames. In fact, I am not even sure they noticed their color or shape. They were just happy to regain the function of one of their senses that they had been missing to some degree or the other.

Sight, in addition to the other four senses, contributes to our overall mental health. It is interesting that four of our five senses (sight, hearing, taste, and smell) are found exclusively in the head area near the brain. This proximity probably explains the robust awareness that we receive from items within our environment. Touch is the only sense found a distance from the brain, and even it is experienced at the head area. Certainly, for those who have lost their sight or from birth have never experienced it, adjustments and an increased awareness of our other senses can occur, which can make up for the difference. Many people who are blind do not consider themselves handicapped. In fact, some may even consider those with physical sight to be the ones who are handicapped because they cannot experience other phases of life to the extent that someone without vision can experience. One of the most beautiful human spirits that I know is found within my friend Jane who is blind. While physical sight is great to possess, even more important is our spiritual (heart) sight. (See Appendix A.)

This Week

This week, I challenge you to take a stroll outside and engage your sense of sight. Look at the colors of nature. Experience how the sense of hearing or smell cause the eyes to turn, without thinking, toward the sound or odor. Think about how quickly the eyes move in all directions without any conscious thought. Ponder about the amazing ability of the eyes to form only one image despite moving your eyes up, down, to the right or left, or even in a circle. Think about how we use this camera known as the eye to help keep us safe and avoid the dangers in our environment. Contemplate why the best camera does not seem to capture all the colors and details of a scene the way that the human eye can. There is something to the statement "You just have to see it to believe it."

Lastly, think about the possible malfunctions that could occur by one of the many moving parts listed above that could result in blurred vision, double vision, or total lack of vision. Then think how fortunate we are that it is the exception rather than the rule for us to experience one of these malfunctions.

That ends a very brief discussion about the eye. Next, I will give you a few eye references that can be found in the Bible. Finally, to end the chapter, I will give you two questions to ponder.

Biblical References to the Eye

The word *eye* is mentioned in the Bible some 560 times. It sometimes refers to the organ itself. Sometimes it refers to understanding. Here are some examples:

- Genesis 3:6: "When the woman (Eve) saw that the fruit of the tree was good for food and pleasing to the *eye*." The camera of our body, known as the eye, creates appealing images within the brain. Those images are then transferred to our heart (spirit) where choices and decisions are made.
- Genesis 6:8: "But Noah found favor (grace) in the *eyes* of the Lord." What? The Lord has eyes? Well, we were created in his image. The "visual" clarity with which the Lord sees, knows, and understands the events of our lives will someday be our own.
- 1 Kings 10:7: "But I did not believe these things until I came and saw with my own *eyes*." The eyes provide a clearer picture of most things than the best description or report.
- Proverbs 30:12: "Those who are pure in their own *eyes* and yet not cleansed of their filth." We can "see" through our eyes with sometimes jaded understanding, or we can see truth through the eyes of our creator.
- Matthew 6:22: "The *eye* is the lamp of the body." N. T. Wright says this about verse 22: "That we must 'keep our eyes on God,'…that we should take care of what we actually look at, and…the eyes are like the headlights of a car. Are your eyes leading you in the right direction and showing you the road ahead?"[8]

- Matthew 7:3: "Why do you look at the speck of sawdust in your brother's *eye*, and pay no attention to the plank in your own *eye*?" The eye is probably the primary sensory organ that we use to begin gathering data in order to judge other people. Often our clarity of vision is hampered by our lack of desire to "see" (understand) God's plan.
- Ephesians 1:18: "I pray that the *eyes* of your heart may be enlightened"—allowing the "eyes" to be open to the entrance point of the inmost self, our heart (spirit), where God's enlightenment can be found and through which we can be formed.
- Hebrews 12:2 "Fixing our *eyes* on Jesus." We are to steadily focus on the story of Jesus in our spiritual walk. You might use this analogy. Like Lewis and Clark, Jesus carved out a path for our journey.

Two Questions about the Eye

First question: What about the eye makes me think that divine creation was involved?

Second question: What about the eye makes me think that it developed by chance?

Below, jot down characteristics that would support both options.

DIVINE DESIGN?	DEVELOPED BY CHANCE?

CHAPTER 4

THE HEART

Four facts about the heart:

1. It has its own mysterious electrical pacemaker that initiates every beat.
2. It beats approximately one hundred thousand times daily.
3. Four valves within the heart open and shut with every beat.
4. It pumps about two thousand gallons of blood daily.

The heart is an organ that rests within the chest cavity and is slightly left of midline. The average heart is the size of an adult's fist. It is a component of a system known as the cardiovascular system. It is represented by the first part of the compound word, *cardiopulmonary*, as in cardiopulmonary resuscitation (CPR). It is the primary organ, should it stop working for some reason, that must be restarted in order to sustain life. Without it, all the other organs within the body would quickly cease to function.

There are a large number of aspects about the heart that could be discussed that would aid in establishing proof that a higher being created us. One of those is the heart's durability. The heart beats approximately 100,000 times daily. (72 beats/minute x 60 minutes/hour x 24 hours/day = 103,680). That amounts to approximately three billion heartbeats that occur in a person with a lifespan of eighty years. For a visual, think about placing a one-dollar bill down every second, including sleep time, for eighty years. Like the eye, we do not consider the effectiveness and durability of the heart.

The heart sounds that are heard in the chest when listening with the stethoscope are created by four valves within the heart. If you think that the cumulative number of heartbeats in an eighty-year-old person is amazing, consider how many times one or the other of the heart valves open and close during that same time. If you were to add all four heart valves, the number would be four hundred thousand times daily. During an eighty-year life span, the cumulative number would be close to twelve billion. Consider a door that you would open every second of the day for eighty years. Would it last? Could a piston in a car engine last eighty years if the engine continuously ran? I am still waiting for someone who can reveal any mechanical manmade object that has that kind of durability.

One of the functions of the heart is to pump blood to all areas of the body. The muscle mass comprising the left ventricle muscle surrounds the larger of the four chambers of the heart. The left ventricle provides the main push for sending the blood to the other body components. The heart pumps two thousand gallons of blood daily through each valve. In a year's time, the heart pumps 730,000 gallons, or 6,570,000 pounds, of blood. The heart not only pumps blood out through the arteries into the remaining parts of the body, it also provides the impetus to return the blood back to the heart in order to continue yet another cycle. As you can see, the heart is an organ of unique muscle tissue that if healthy continues to work for years without seeming to tire as do other muscles of the body.

The different areas of the heart muscle contract in sequence with one another. The four heart chambers are filled and then emptied at the appropriate time to provide a consistent flow of blood through the heart and then to all parts of the body. Each time that the heart contracts, representing one heartbeat, blood is transferred through the heart in a repetitive sequence. Blood flows from the inferior and superior vena cava (two large veins that carry the blood back to the heart after the body has used the oxygen provided it) into the right atrium of the heart, through the atrial valve, into the right ventricle, through the pulmonary valve, into the lungs to replenish oxygen in the blood, through the pulmonary artery, into the left atrium, through the mitral valve, into the left ventricle, through the aortic valve, into the aortic artery, and then to other parts of the body. After this, the blood returns back to the vena cava, and the cycle repeats itself. (See Image 2.)

Because the heart is a muscle, it too needs oxygen-rich blood flow. The heart provides its own oxygen containing blood that flows through arteries located on the outside of the heart known as coronary arteries. These coronary arteries have smaller arterioles that dive into the heart muscle and provide the oxygen and nourishment needed. Think of the heart as an organ that provides its own fuel (with a little help from the lungs, of course). The coronary arteries are the arteries that can become blocked with a blood clot or the effects of the products related to a high concentration of lipids within the blood. When the blood flow is impeded to the heart muscle, it can produce damage to the heart muscle known as a myocardial infarction, or heart attack.

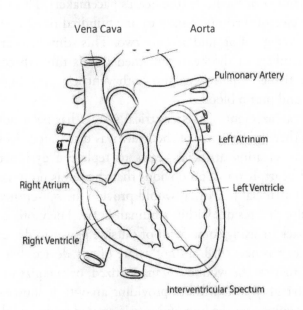

Image 2: The Human Heart

Some data suggest that the most common day for heart attacks is Monday, so try to avoid being overly stressed on the first day back from the weekend. Laughing seems to be good for the heart. Try to find something that makes you laugh on Mondays as well as other days. The most common day of the year for heart attacks is Christmas Day. This likely is due to eating a larger meal that requires blood, to some degree, to be diverted or "stolen" from the heart and sent to the gastrointestinal system to help aid in the digestion of the larger meal. There are also other possible factors involved in both days.

The Heart's Generator

The most intriguing component of the heart is its indwelling pacemaker and electrical system that continuously self-generates a heartbeat. Initiating each beat is not a conscious decision. Can you imagine if it was? That would be an impossibility unless we did not sleep.

The heartbeat originates from a small mass of tissue in the right upper chamber of the heart (the heart's pacemaker). This tissue generates an electrical stimulus sixty to one hundred times each minute with an average of around seventy-two. This stimulus starts in the upper chambers of the heart and then travels through conductive nervelike tissue or pathways into both ventricles, causing them to contract and pump blood.

The amazement of this electrical system has been noted from the time that the function of the heart was discovered. As scientists worked on creating artificial hearts to replace a dysfunctional or damaged heart, it was soon obvious that there was nothing to place within an artificial heart that would provide the self-created electrical impulse that resides within a human heart. Therefore, carrying a battery pack or using some form of outside power to drive the artificial heart was needed. I am not aware of any device that man has invented that can be wound up, magnetized, or energized to last for seventy to eighty years without providing an outside source of power to keep it going. Yet the human heart is created to do just that.

The heart is part of the cardiovascular system. The vascular component of this system refers to the arteries that carry the blood away from the heart and the veins that carry blood back to the heart. If you were to stretch out all of the blood vessels within one human body, including the capillaries that connect the arteries to the veins, it would run some 60,000 miles.

The arteries carry oxygen-rich blood that has passed through the lungs where it rids the body of carbon dioxide and enriches with oxygen. The oxygen-enriched blood flows into smaller and smaller arteries until it reaches our muscles and other organs that require oxygen in order to function. Those muscles and other organs then withdraw the oxygen and exchange it with carbon dioxide as the blood returns back through smaller veins to reach larger veins. These larger veins return the oxygen-deprived blood to the right side of the heart into the lungs to repeat the process over and over.

The components of the blood that travel daily through these 60,000 miles of blood vessels are interesting as well. The plasma is the liquid part of blood. The blood cells that do all the work are produced in the bone marrow. The bone marrow is the soft spongy material in the center of the bone. It produces red blood cells, white blood cells, and platelets. The red blood cells carry oxygen to the tissues and carries carbon dioxide away from the tissues and back to the lungs where it can be discarded. The white blood cells help fight against bacteria and other infectious agents in order to aid our immune system. They also aid in healing wounds by cleaning up debris and dead cells within the wound itself. Platelets release substances that help in the blood clotting process which helps to control bleeding.

In addition to carrying oxygen, blood carries electrolytes, antibodies, vitamins, heat, and nourishment to the body tissues. It also carries waste matter along with the carbon dioxide away from human tissue. The production and function of blood is very complex but is a process that "works behind the scenes" in order to keep us healthy.

Blood Clotting

An event that has or potentially will save our lives multiple times during our life span is the blood-clotting process. Blood clotting is another amazing process that takes place in our body behind the scenes but in one sense also takes place in front of our very eyes. The platelets, red blood cells, and white blood cells that have already been mentioned share space in the blood with clotting factors. These blood-clotting factors constantly circulate in the blood stream and stand ready to assist us not unlike a soldier guard.

What happens when we cut ourselves with a knife or are involved in an accident that can lead to loss of blood? How does the blood loss slow down and then stop? Blood clotting is a process that requires multiple steps. The process begins as the blood vessels begin to spasm or decrease in size. Platelets begin to adhere around the site of bleeding. A process known as the clotting cascade is triggered (Image 3).

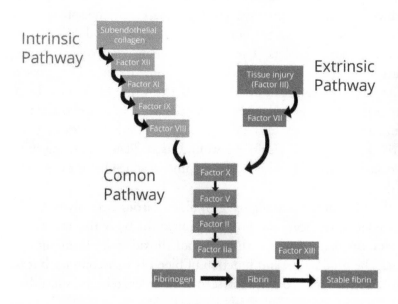

Image 3: Blood-Clotting Cascade

The blood clotting cascade is a biochemical process that is carried out by our body in a very precise way. The process consists of proteins already circulating within the blood stream. The major proteins involved are numbered using roman numerals II–XIII. Many of these proteins activate another protein within the cascade to form a product that helps in the clotting process sequence with the common goal of providing fibrin. Fibrin is an insoluble protein formed from the fibrinogen being acted upon by factor IIa, and then fibrin is acted upon by factor XIII, which forms a stable fibrous mesh similar to a patch that impedes the flow of blood.

To briefly summarize this process, think about what happens when you cut your finger and the blood begins to pour out. The blood vessel "spasms," or narrows, to help slow the flow of blood. Platelets, which are sticky and circulate in the blood, adhere to the cut area of the blood vessel to begin to slow the flow. These platelets release a chemical that activates the products of the clotting cascade. Then the thirteen factors of the clotting cascade do their thing in forming the fibrin mesh or patch that stops the bleeding until the skin and blood vessels have a chance to repair themselves. (In chapter 6, I will discuss how the skin repairs itself back to a normal appearance even when a significant piece of skin is missing following trauma—another amazing feat.)

This Week

At work or school this week, consider how little you are aware of your heart's activity. When things are going well, you probably do not even sense that the heart is functioning in a way that is providing the circulation of blood, removing impurities such as carbon dioxide from the body, and maintaining your blood pressure at a constant level so that you don't faint. The heart and blood vessels automatically adjust if your blood pressure gets too low and help to prevent a stroke if it begins to get too high. Like most functions of the body, consider why you don't have to think about how to make your heart beat, how to make it pump just the right amount of blood, or how to make new blood cells. The heart, which is so vital to life here on earth, is an organ that is durable, consistent, and has its own ignition system (the heart's pacemaker) that cannot be matched by any human creator.

This week, see if you can find your pulse in the wrist area just before you get to the thumb area. Count the number of beats per minute. From that number, calculate the number of beats in a day, a week, a month, a year, and a lifetime. As you do this, try to think of any man-made mechanical device that might be even ten percent as durable or consistent as the heart. Reflect on both the muscle durability of the organ and the valves inside as you think about the three billion beats.

That is the information I wanted to share about the cardiovascular system, the blood and some of its ingredients, as well as the biochemical reactions that occur. In the next chapter, I would like to share some thoughts about the second component of the compound word *cardiopulmonary*. In cardiopulmonary resuscitation, CPR, the lungs are the most important organ to revive after the heart.

Biblical References to the Heart

If for some reason you forget to reveal your compassion to someone and they question whether or not you have a heart, you can retort by saying, "Not only do I have a heart, but I have two." There are 725 biblical references to the heart. Virtually all of those references do not refer to the function of the human heart muscle but refers to the deep inner core of reasoning, choice, and decision-making. I like Dallas Willard's definition of the heart, also known as the spirit or will:

> Heart refers to its position in the human being, as the center or core to which every other component of the self owes its proper functioning.

He goes on to say,

> The human heart, will, or spirit is the executive center of a human life. The heart is where decisions and choices are made for the whole person. That is its function.[9]

The heart that Willard is referring to is not the brain. We will differentiate the two in chapters 8, the conclusion, and in Appendix A. The other heart mentioned only a few times in the Bible is the physical, blood-pumping organ.

An example of a verse referring to the human heart muscle is found in Exodus 28:29:

> Whenever Aaron enters the Holy Place, he will bear the names of the sons of Israel over his heart on the breast piece of decision as a continuing memorial before the Lord.

This is one of the rare exceptions where the Bible refers to the organ that we refer to as the physical heart muscle.

To see biblical examples of the heart as it refers to the human spirit, will, or choice, see Appendix A. We will uncover some of the functions of this important part of our being in chapters 8 and the conclusion.

Two Questions about the Heart

First question: What about the heart makes me think that divine creation was involved?

Second question: What about the heart makes me think that it developed by chance?

Below, jot down characteristics that would support both options.

DIVINE DESIGN?   DEVELOPED BY CHANCE?

CHAPTER 5

THE LUNGS

Four facts about the lungs:

1. Exchanges oxygen for carbon dioxide waste in the six hundred million alveoli.
2. Your lungs are the only organs that can float.
3. No need to remember to breathe because your lungs are controlled by your brain.
4. A yawn occurs when your brain senses low oxygen.

The lungs are organs that rest within the chest cavity. (See Image 4.) The right and left lungs are connected to each other by the bronchial tree. They lie on either side of the heart. They are the second component of a system known as the cardiopulmonary system. They are crucial components of life-sustaining importance. Like the heart, should they stop working for any reason, life would be unsustainable without outside intervention. Like the heart, without functioning lungs, all of the other organs within the body would quickly cease to function.

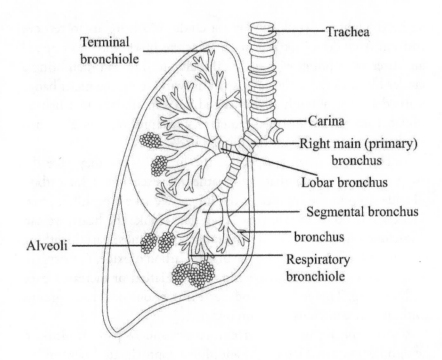

Image 4: Right Lung, Trachea, and Bronchus

An interesting fact about the lungs is that there are three lobes (segments) in the right lung and only two lobes in the left lung. The heart rests more in the left chest cavity and most likely accounts for less space for the left lung. Despite the difference in number of lobes, each lung functions in the same way.

Another interesting fact about the lungs is that they are the only organs within the human body that float. Even on deep exhalation, there is enough air left for them to float. This is a very helpful fact during water rescues. The aerated lungs aid in the opportunity to get someone to the surface quicker and be transported out of the water without feeling the downward pull of the person's body weight. I witnessed this fact when I was at scout camp in my early teens, working on my lifesaving merit badge. One of the exercises to complete the merit badge was to retrieve an aerated weighted dummy from the bottom of the lake at a depth of about ten feet. At that time, my instructor said that he was unable to find one of the dummies, so he thought he would just use a cinder block for us to retrieve instead. A cinder block is a heavy concrete block with no trapped air. After attempting, with great difficulty, to find and then bring a cinder block to the surface, those of us working on the merit badge learned a lesson about how the aerated lungs in humans are a help in rescue. I am sure my instructor knew that fact previously and was just teaching us a lesson about the human body.

The most amazing aspect of the lungs is how they take the oxygen out of the air that we breathe and exchange it for carbon dioxide deep in the recesses of the lungs. We take a breath approximately 16,000 to 18,000 times each day. Unlike the heart, we can consciously make ourselves breathe; but for the most part, breathing is "automatic," controlled by the brain. Carbon dioxide, not oxygen, is the main chemical for triggering the initiation or increased pace of breathing. This in turn produces contractions of muscle groups without any conscious effort on our part.

Atmospheric air is 21 percent oxygen and 78 percent nitrogen with other gases making up the additional approximate 1 percent. As we breathe in, air moves down the trachea, into the bronchial tree, and into the alveoli. There are approximately six hundred million alveoli. (See Image 5.) Think of the alveoli as a tiny berry-shaped balloon or soap bubble on the end of a tiny straw. The alveoli are so small that they cannot be seen by the naked eye. Their walls consist of a thin membrane that is 0.5 microns in thickness (about two hundred of these walls stacked together would equal the width of a grain of salt). The alveoli walls rest against the capillary blood vessel walls. The oxygen and carbon dioxide passes through these walls in an exchange process. The oxygen concentration is higher on the lung alveoli side which allows oxygen to transfer into the capillary while the carbon dioxide is higher in concentration on the capillary side, allowing it to transfer into the alveoli to be exhaled as we breathe out. Inhaled air has approximately 21 percent oxygen saturation while exhaled air has approximately 15 to 16 percent oxygen in addition to the discarded carbon dioxide that is being expelled.

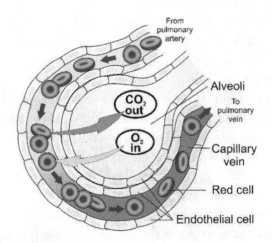

Image 5: Alveolus

As oxygen enters the alveoli and passes into the capillaries, it attaches to the hemoglobin of the red blood cell. Only about 1 to 2 percent of oxygen is dissolved directly into blood. The remaining 98 percent is attached to the iron-containing portion of the hemoglobin. These red blood cells then are transported to organs and other living tissues where the oxygen is extracted and utilized to make ATP. This process provides energy or fuel to allow the body to function. In general, as the oxygen concentration increases to a certain level, so does the ATP production, which is used by each cell of the body to perform a process known as cellular respiration. (See chapter 2—Kreb's cycle and cellular respiration.) As energy is produced, carbon dioxide is produced by the organs and tissues. This carbon dioxide, which is an important side product of the Kreb's cycle, then reenters the capillaries to be transported to the alveoli to be expelled by the lungs. There is some truth that talking to your plants could help them flourish as plants require carbon dioxide in order to complete a process known as photosynthesis.

Someone might think if 21 percent oxygen is good, 100 percent oxygen would be even better. However, in a normal lung, 100 percent oxygen can damage the cells that line the alveoli. This can cause a fluid abnormality in the alveoli, causing an abnormal exchange of gases leading to an increased breathing pattern and imbalance. This can produce damage to the heart, lungs, and brain. It is amazing that the human body is made in such a way that the exact atmospheric gases match the exact need for lung exchange of gases to provide for the body's organs to function.

Another function of the lungs is to provide air to cross the vocal cords in order to speak and make sounds. Try speaking without exhaling with the lungs. If sounds are made at all, they sound different. The vocal cords are found in the larynx of the neck and are attached to the thyroid cartilage, or as we may know it, the Adam's apple. The vocal cords produce speech and sound when they come together and then vibrate as air passes through them during the exhalation phase. The pitch of the voice is determined by how quickly the vocal cords vibrate. In order for your voice to be clear, the vocal cords must vibrate symmetrically and with the same frequency.

The lungs also work to some degree as a filter. The trachea and bronchial tubes have an escalator, or elevator, that transports the inhaled, unwanted items back to the throat to be swallowed or expelled. Each breath we take exposes the lungs to the outside environment which contains things such as pollen, germs, dust, and even insects that can pose a threat to our health. Mucus that is produced by cells in the respiratory tract traps these potentially dangerous materials. Then cilia, which line a large part of the upper respiratory tubes, transport this mucus and the materials stuck to it by using wavelike motions to send it to an area to be cleared.

This Week

As you go about this week, think about this simple thing called breathing that requires a complex number of events to occur that include the alveoli (six hundred million of them), capillaries, hemoglobin, oxygen-carbon dioxide exchange, and breathable oxygen that is 21 percent in the atmosphere. The lungs, like many of the other organs, reveal irreducible complexity. You could not survive by "reducing" them down to just the lungs without the blood vessels, blood components, and oxygen extraction. If you did, the lungs would not work. Without the coordination of the multiple steps listed above, the lungs would not be able to perform their function of getting oxygen to the distal parts of the body. Think about air going through the vocal cords to allow you to speak. Try to speak, sing, or yell without air from the lungs crossing through the vocal cords. Think about the lungs being a "paired" organ like the kidneys or the eyes. This allows for the flexibility to continue to live even when one lung is damaged or has to be removed because of trauma or disease.

Biblical References to the Lungs

The actual word *lung* is not found in the RSV Bible.

The word *breath* is used some seventy-nine times in the Bible. Some examples:

- Genesis 2:7: "Then the Lord God formed a man from the dust of the ground and *breathed* into his nostrils the *breath* of life, and the man became a living being."
- Genesis 25:8: "Then Abraham *breathed* his last and died at a good old age, an old man and full of years; and he was gathered to his people." "Breathed his/her last" referred to death. When we stop breathing, death follows in a few short minutes.
- Exodus 15:10: "But you (God) blew with your *breath*, and the sea covered them. They sank like lead in the mighty waters." God's breath provided a saving grace for the Hebrew people as this verse refers to the waters of the Red Sea coming together to destroy the Egyptians during the Exodus.
- Job 7:7: "Remember, O God, that my life is but a *breath*; my eyes will never see happiness again." The brevity of life compared to eternity is spoken of as life being "but a breath."
- Job 32:8. "But it is the spirit in a person, the *breath* of the Almighty, that gives me life." The spirit is often referred to as "wind" or "the breath of the Almighty." We will cover more on the spirit in later chapters.

- Psalm 150:6. "Let everything that has *breath* praise the Lord." Our lungs (breath) play a role in praising the Lord as discussed above when looking at the functions of the vocal cords.
- Mark 15:37. "With a loud cry, Jesus *breathed* his last." The incarnate son of God, Jesus, experienced the same earthly death that is our destiny unless Jesus comes first.
- Acts 9:1. "Meanwhile, Saul was still *breathing* out murderous threats against the Lord's disciples." Our breath can be used for words for the good of others or as threats.
- 2 Timothy 3:16. "All scripture is God-*breathed* and is useful for teaching, rebuking, correcting and training in righteousness." N. T. Wright commented this about 2 Timothy 3:16: "The Spirit who caused it to be written, who spoke through the different writers in so many ways, is as powerful today as ever, and that power, through the written word, can transform lives."[10]

Two Questions about the Lungs

First question: What about the lungs make me think that divine creation was involved?

Second question: What about the lungs make me think that it developed by chance?

Below, jot down characteristics that would support both options.

DIVINE DESIGN?   DEVELOPED BY CHANCE?

CHAPTER 6

THE SKIN

Four facts about the skin:

1. It repairs and at times replaces itself within two to six weeks.
2. It sweats to keep from overheating.
3. It keeps bacteria from entering the body.
4. It warns you when you touch something hot or cold.

If the eye is known as one of the most complex organs of the human body and the heart and lungs are known as the most critical organs for sustaining life, the organ known as the skin should get the nod for its durability and toughness. Yes, I did say that the skin is an organ. In fact, it is the largest organ of the body. The skin is a multi-layered, thin organ that has many unique features such as its ability to repair itself, regulate aspects of the body which allow the other organs to function properly, and provides a defense system much like the armor of a gladiator.

The skin consists of three layers of tissue: the upper epidermis layer, middle dermis layer, and the lower hypodermis (fatty tissue) layer. (See image 6.) It contains sweat glands, blood vessels, hair follicles, and nerve endings. Each of these items perform a specific function that is important to the longevity of our entire being.

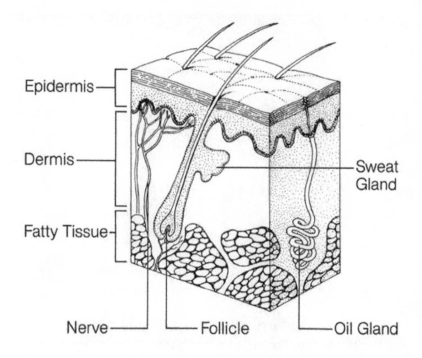

Image 6: The Skin (Source: National Cancer
Institute; creator: unknown illustrator)

I will discuss the interesting protective functions of the components of the skin later in this chapter. First, I would like to share what may be the most amazing aspect of the skin that each of us have seen "firsthand" but probably taken for granted. That is the amazing wound repair or regeneration.

My Hand's New Addition

Last fall, I was using a grinder to sharpen my lawnmower blade. As I was sharpening and positioning the blade on the grinder, the "middle knuckle" (also known as the proximal interphalangeal joint) of my right middle finger seemed to get in the way of the rotating grinding wheel. Needless to say, the skin on my finger was no match for the grinding wheel. It did not even slow it down. As is often the case with trauma to the skin, it took a fraction of a second to realize that I had made a mistake. About the time the nerves in my finger sent the impulse to and from the brain to remind me, the sense of smell kicked in as well with the odor of burning skin. When I withdrew my finger, I was left with a missing small chunk of skin. It was not like a cut, where the two sides of the cut can be approximated and sutured together. A chunk of my skin was missing in action. Because of the heat from the grinder, I guess you could say that the skin went up in smoke. At least I could not find any pieces around the grinder.

Most of us have had one or more episodes of scraping a knee or losing the surface of an even deeper area of the skin only to see it repair itself over days to weeks. There are two main kinds of skin or wound healing: healing by primary intention and healing by secondary intention. Primary intention refers to the healing of the skin when it has been damaged because of a cut or laceration. This type of healing occurs when there has been very little tissue loss. The new blood vessels and cells that make new skin only have a small distance to migrate in order to heal the area. The skin edges are approximated by a Band-Aid, Steri-Strips, or sutures while the process of healing occurs.

Healing by secondary intention is nothing short of a miracle. It occurs when there is an open wound with loss of cells or tissue and the sides of the lesion cannot be approximated or "brought together." I would like to spend a little time discussing healing and skin regeneration by secondary intention. That is the type of healing that was required to replace the chunk of skin on my finger that was missing in action.

When skin is injured and the process of secondary intention begins, the body sets in motion a number of events known as the "cascade of healing." This cascade involves four distinct healing phases. (See image 7.)

Phase one is the bleeding phase. The objective of this phase is to stop the bleeding. In this phase, the body kicks in its 911 system to activate the blood-clotting system. The blood vessels constrict, the platelets within our blood activate and adhere to the wounded area, and the clotting mechanism begins to form a fibrin mesh which strengthens the clumps of platelets, resulting in an eventual stable clot. (See chapter 4—blood clotting.)

The second phase is the inflammatory phase. During this phase, white blood cells known as neutrophils enter the base of the wound to destroy any bacteria and clean the wound by removing debris (similar to Pac-Man). After about two days, the neutrophils leave and are replaced by specialized white blood cells known as macrophages. *Macro* means large. These large white blood cells continue to clear the debris. They also secrete proteins and growth-enhancing ingredients that attract immune system cells to come to the wound to aid in tissue repair. This phase may last four to seven days. It is often associated with redness, swelling, and heat at the site of injury.

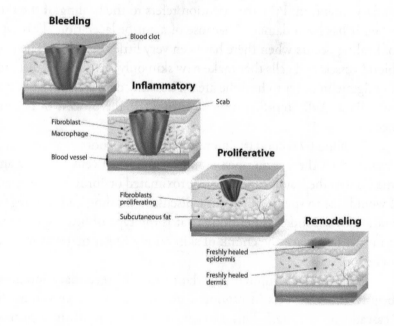

Image 7: Wound-Healing Process

After the neutrophils and macrophages do their thing, it leads to the third phase, known as the proliferative phase. During it, deep red granulation tissue fills the wound bed with connective tissue along with the formation of new blood vessels. Cells known as fibroblast help to break down the fibrin clot which helped stop the bleeding in phase one. They also create new extracellular matrix and collagen to support the other cells that are involved in the healing. During this time, the wound margins contract and start to pull toward the center of the wound. After this, epithelial cells arise from the wound bed or margins (or both) and begin to move across the wound bed until it is covered with epithelium. The proliferative phase can last as long as three weeks.

During the last or remodeling phase, the newly formed tissue gains strength and the ability to stretch. Stretchy collagen fibers reorganize, the tissue continues to remodel and mature until it regains about three-fourths of its original tensile strength. This last phase can last from weeks to a couple of years.

What an amazing process. Tissue that was damaged and no longer present is replaced without any "outside" help except for providing good nutrition and avoiding infection. The other interesting aspect is that the newly formed skin looks basically the same as the previous skin. There may be some differences in appearance if the wound or loss of skin is large. Remember my clumsy attempt at sharpening my mower blade? After about three months, you have to look extremely close to tell the difference between it and my other noninjured hand joints.

Some larger areas of trauma where skin is missing may be treated with skin flaps (part of the skin near the wound/injury is undermined, released, and rotated into the area of absent skin) or by skin grafts where a layer of skin is removed from one part of the body and transferred to the area of need. With skin grafts, the body amazingly repairs the epidermis and other tissues where the skin graft was taken. Scientists' attempts to create a product to replace needed skin in an individual have been dismal. Collagen products and artificial coverings in an attempt to speed the natural healing process have at times been detrimental to healing or caused additional complications.

I hope you agree that healing of skin is one of the wonders of the body in which there are many. How can something be made from nothing? Also, what keeps the process from continuing once the skin is replaced? If there were no controls of the healing process set in motion, the healing area would continue to grow, producing a large lump or mound of skin. Can you imagine a skin avulsion on the nose or the back that would continue being replaced by skin and the other materials that help to restore a damaged area? You might end up with something like Pinocchio or the Hunchback of Notre Dame if the body was not created in a way that shut down the skin reproductive process once the healing is completed.

Dealing with the Heat

How does the body remain at or near 98.6 degrees on a hot day? It is through the utilization of approximately two to four million sweat glands located in our skin. (See image 6 earlier in chapter.) Sweating is controlled by a center in the hypothalamic portion of the brain. As the skin temperature starts to rise, sweating occurs in a response to produce a decrease in the body's temperature. As sweat is produced, evaporative cooling takes place as air passes over the surface of the skin. The skin and superficial blood vessels decrease in temperature. The cooled venous blood is sent back to the core of the body to counter rises in overall core temperature.

In addition to sweating from overheating, sweat can be produced by emotional stress. Most of emotional-stress sweating is limited to certain areas of the body such as the palms, armpits, soles of the feet, and the forehead.

There are 2 different types of sweat glands found in humans. One is the eccrine gland. The eccrine glands are responsible for the majority of the thermoregulation (dispersing body heat) of the body. Sweat is mostly water. Sodium is one of the main minerals within sweat along with smaller amounts of potassium, calcium, and magnesium. Some people may sweat as much as two to three liters each hour during the right climate conditions with a total daily volume close to twelve to fourteen liters. It is more difficult to "cool down" when the air humidity is high. This is because the sweat on the skin surface does not have a way of evaporating as quickly because the atmospheric air is more saturated with water. This is why the body is at greater risk for heat exhaustion or even heatstroke during days with higher humidity.

A second type of sweat gland is known as the apocrine gland. These glands are found mainly in the armpits and a few other areas. They produce more of an oily secretion that is initially nonodorous but when combined with bacteria that is on the surface of the skin produces a decomposition material that gives it the characteristic odor known as "body odor," or "BO."

Another safeguard that the skin provides the human body is that of announcing that a potential harmful insult is coming in contact with it. The skin has millions of sensory nerve endings. These nerve endings warn us by announcing that abnormal heat or cold items are in contact with our body. These "bare" afferent nerve endings send a signal to the brain. The signal from the brain goes through efferent nerve fibers to a muscle group, producing withdrawal of that part of the body from the insult. Therefore, if we did not have this system in place, we would have severe burns from touching items that were hot or experience problems such as frostbite before we noticed the sensation or the degree of cold.

Although the skin functions in a remarkable way in order to protect us from heat, that protection can be overridden by prolonged exposure to heat and dehydration. Heatstroke is an emergency situation in which the sweat glands shut down and the body cannot release heat. It may start as a progression from symptoms such as leg cramps and fainting. You are usually still sweating at the time of this "heat exhaustion." If you are not cooled and rehydrated, it can lead to an increase in the core body temperature to greater than 104 degrees and have associated symptoms such as seizures, confusion, disorientation, and coma. Again, heatstroke is an emergency situation that warrants a 911 call followed by first aid until the first responders arrive.

For this upcoming week, think back to an accident that left you with missing skin somewhere on your body, possibly missing it from a knee hitting the asphalt, slicing a cardboard box with a box knife only to find that you sliced skin off your hand as well, or flying over the handlebars of your bike, faceplanting into gravel. I have done all these and many more. Now try to find the area where you lost the skin. Chances are if you look closely, you may find a small scar, but imagine the divots that would be present if it were not for this miraculous skin repair system.

Also, think of the times outdoors or indoors that would have not been possible without the cooling system of the skin. Playing the great game of baseball or even watching another sporting event would be impossible during the summer months in most states without a functional sweating system. Because of our skin, we can enjoy work and play without overheating and without carrying cooling blankets that we would have to use frequently during the day.

Think about when you wrap your hand around a cold drink. Think how it gives you a good vibe in the summer to cool you down but may make you shiver in the winter. Think about the times when you withdrew your hand as you touched something that was very hot or cold. Without these nerve fibers working correctly in your hands or other parts of the body, the skin would deteriorate, which would interrupt your primary defense system.

Biblical References to the Skin

Skin is referred in the Bible some eighty times. A large number of these, including all references in the New Testament, refer to animal skins that were dried and used for containers to carry water or wine.

The Old Testament book with the majority of references to human skin is Leviticus. In Leviticus chapters 11 through 15, God gave instructions about what foods to avoid, how to handle skin diseases, time references after childbirth, and how to handle bodily discharges in order to keep his chosen people, the Israelites, healthy. You might say that Leviticus reveals guides that God gave which are similar to what would be given by our current-day county health departments. These instructions to prevent spread of disease occurred thousands of years before Antoni van Leeuwenhoek even discovered bacteria. It seems obvious to me that God has always been all knowing. Here are some examples of skin precautions: (See chapter 7 for guidelines given for food consumption.)

- Leviticus 13:2: "When anyone has a swelling or a rash or a shiny spot on their *skin* that may be a defiling *skin* disease, they must be brought to Aaron the priest or to one of his sons who is a priest." Many of the Hebrew people were pronounced as unclean or required to isolate or be quarantined for a period of time to prevent spread of disease.
- Leviticus 13:3: "And the sore appears to be more than *skin* deep, it is a defiling skin disease."
- Leviticus 13:4: "If the shiny spot on the *skin* is white but does not appear to be more than *skin* deep and the hair in it has not turned white, the priest is to isolate the affected person for seven days." On the seventh day, the priest would examine them again; and if the sore had faded and had not spread in the skin, the priest would pronounce them clean, stating that it was only a rash.
- Leviticus 13:10–11: "The priest is to examine them and if there is a white swelling in the *skin* that has turned the hair white and if there is raw flesh in the swelling, it is a chronic *skin* disease and the priest shall pronounce them unclean. He is not to isolate them, because they are already unclean." An unclean person had to avoid places considered holy. Being considered unclean placed the person in "harm's way" at times. Some, such as lepers, were expulsed from their land, had to pronounce that they were unclean when a certain distance from others, and lived lives of isolation.
- Leviticus 13:24–25: "When someone has a burn on their *skin* and a reddish-white or white spot appears in the raw flesh of the burn…and it appears to be more than *skin* deep, it is a defiling disease that has broken out of the burn."

Here are some others referring to human skin:

- Genesis 27:11: "Jacob said to Rebekah his mother, 'But my brother Esau is a hairy man while I have smooth *skin*.'" From the beginning, our skin was different between different individuals.
- Job 2:4: "*Skin* for *skin*!" Satan replied. "A man will give all he has for his own life."
- Psalm 102:5: "In my distress I groan aloud and am reduced to *skin* and bones." Skin and bones refer to loss of weight, including muscle, that sometimes occurs under stress.
- Numbers 5:2: "Command the Israelites to send away from the camp anyone who has a defiling *skin* disease or a discharge of any kind, or who is ceremonially unclean because of a dead body."

Two Questions about the Skin

First question: What about the skin makes me think that divine creation was involved?

Second question: What about the skin makes me think that it developed by chance?

Below, jot down characteristics that would support both options.

DIVINE DESIGN?	DEVELOPED BY CHANCE?

Chapter 7

The Digestive System

Four facts about the digestive system:

1. You produce about one quart of saliva daily.
2. Gas forms in the large intestine when bacteria ferment carbohydrates that aren't digested in your small intestine.
3. The acid in your stomach is strong enough to burn your skin.
4. There are "good" bacteria that aid in your health within the intestine.

The digestive system is one of the organ systems that is not a frequent conversation piece at most get-togethers or parties. However, it is one of the most inconvenient ones when it is not functioning well. All of us have had some degree of dysfunction of the digestive system, leading to nausea, vomiting, diarrhea, fever, cramps, and multiple other symptoms.

How do we maintain normal bowel function? How does the food that we eat turn into the nutrients that the body needs to provide fuel, growth, and repair of our cells which in many cases are needed to survive? How does the body decide what is not needed and discard the remainder in our stool or bowel movement? How are the different functions of the digestive system affected by stress, anxiety, depression, and other emotional factors? Do we require three square meals a day in order to remain healthy? What does it mean when we say you need a "well-balanced meal"? There are as many questions about the bowel and its function as there are questions about most any other organ.

Whether you start with an apple, your favorite steak, or some other food, the ingredients are extracted from each in a very precise way to provide nutrients that the body needs or does not need (when we eat too much of a food, the body often lets us know of our poor choice by one of multiple symptoms or by witnessing weight gain). This precision occurs over and over again on a daily basis. When the digestive system is working well and we are consistent with the types of food we eat, the amount of stress we face, and many other factors, it remains remarkably consistent in its function. In this setting, frequency of bowel movements, lack of pain or cramping, and the timeline for feeling the next hunger pains can be approximated fairly accurately.

However, like most other organs or organ systems in the body, a tiny change in the function of the organ, changes in the biochemical reactions associated with the organ's function, or an injury to that organ can cause life changes on a multitude of levels. Unfortunately, most of us continue to take God's greatest creation, our bodies, for granted until they are malfunctioning.

The digestive tract is a long tube with twists and turns that begins at the mouth and ends at the anus. (See image 8.) It contains a series of muscles that move the food and ingredients through the tract by a wavelike motion known as peristalsis. Along the way, different enzymes and hormones aid in the breakdown of food and release of the important nutrients. The digestion is aided by other accessory organs that take part in the process.

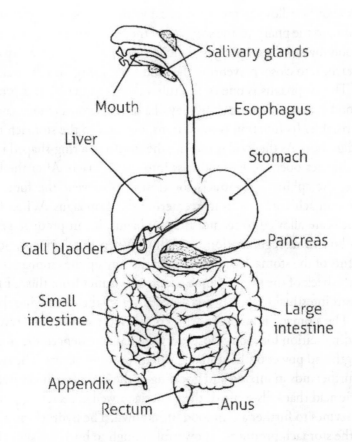

Image 8: The Digestive System

Digestion begins in the mouth. Before food even touches the mouth, digestion is often engaged by the smell of food, which produces saliva that contains enzymes that are on the ready to break down food. Saliva increases when the food comes in contact with the mouth. We then use our teeth (grinders) to chew the food thoroughly to help in the initial process of digestion.

After the initial breakdown of the food from chewing and the enzymes of the saliva, the food passes into the esophagus. This requires swallowing which, for the most part, is an involuntary reflex, although it can occur voluntarily. The majority of the time, we don't think about swallowing the quart of saliva that we produce daily. The tongue and the pharynx, the soft part of the back of the mouth, pushes the food toward the esophagus, which causes the epiglottis, a flap over the trachea, to close, preventing the food from going into the trachea.

The esophagus is one of the tubes that is muscular and propels the food toward the stomach by way of a series of contractions known as peristalsis. Its function is more transportation to the stomach than it is digestion. As the food is nearing the stomach, a ring-shaped muscle sphincter opens to let food pass into the stomach. After the food passes, the sphincter contracts, or closes, to prevent the food and other stomach contents from reentering the esophagus. When food and acid are allowed to reenter the esophagus, it can produce symptoms known as regurgitation, or reflux. When this happens, acidic contents of the stomach can make it all the way up the esophagus and into the back of the throat. Some people may suffer from this GERD, or gastrointestinal reflux disease, especially at night when lying flat.

The stomach is an organ with considerable power that serves as a holding station for food. Most everyone has experienced the muscle strength and power of the stomach when vomiting occurs. The stomach further aids in mixing and grinding of the food. It secretes hydrochloric acid that kills some of the bacteria as well as secreting powerful enzymes to further aid in food breakdown. The hydrochloric acid that the stomach produces is powerful enough to burn the skin. This is another example of how the body is created with a tough lining in this part of the system. This acid is necessary in order to kill the bacteria that is present in most all of our food in addition to bacteria that resides on the hands of small children who frequently place their hands in their mouths. By the time food exits the stomach, changes have occurred, producing a consistency of a soft material or liquid.

Food now moves into the small intestine. It consists of three segments—the duodenum, jejunum, and the ileum. The duodenum receives enzymes from the pancreas as well as bile from the liver and the gallbladder. The gallbladder is a collecting bag which stores bile and squeezes or pushes the bile out into the bile duct and then into the duodenum. The gallbladder squeezes harder the larger the meal or the higher the fat content within the meal. This can produce the pain experienced in the right upper abdomen if you have formed gallstones within the gallbladder. The term for gallstones within the gallbladder is cholelithiasis. The pancreas duct and the bile duct share the same entrance port into the duodenum. The bile duct, the pancreas duct, or the common port used by both, can become blocked, producing significant symptoms. Blockage of the pancreatic duct can cause severe life-threatening symptoms due to the pancreas enzymes attacking the pancreas itself, causing pancreatitis.

Food is also moved through the stomach by peristalsis. The duodenum continues to break down the food along with mixing in the bile and enzymes mentioned above. The jejunum and ileum are mainly responsible for absorption of nutrients into the blood to be transported to cells throughout the body. By this point, the food has been broken down into carbohydrates, protein, fats, and vitamins. Vitamins are classified into those that dissolve in water (water-soluble vitamins) and those that absorb into fat (fat-soluble vitamins). The digestive process further breaks these foods down into products such as sugars, amino acids, fatty acids, and glycerol. Following this, these broken-down products enter the blood stream and are transported to the cells of the body. Cells have three ways to make energy (ATP) within the cell. Remember the Kreb's cycle in chapter 2? That is one of them. The other two are glycolysis and oxidative phosphorylation. All three of these processes use energy-rich molecules in order to generate ATP, which provides energy for the human cells and, therefore, energy to use our muscles and make other organs function.

This process of intestinal motility involves the activity of a large number of hormones (some of which come from the pancreas), muscles, and nerves. After continued digestive activity, and nutrients are absorbed, the remainder of the food products move into the large intestine, or colon, to continue in the process. Everything above the colon is known as the upper GI tract. The remainder below is known as the lower GI tract.

The large intestine, or colon, is five to six feet long. It is the muscular tube that connects the ileum to the rectum. It consists of the cecum, ascending colon (including the appendix), transverse colon, descending colon, and sigmoid colon, which connects to the rectum. As the residual contents of food passes through the colon, any remaining water is absorbed, and the waste is processed to provide, hopefully, a convenient time for excretion. It normally takes about thirty-six hours for food to transport through the colon. A large percent of the residual stool is made up of food debris and fiber as well as bacteria. These bacteria are not harmful and often are protective to the body. They help in the formation of some vitamins, help in continuing to process the food waste products, and protect against harmful bacteria. It is not uncommon for a bacteria-like Clostridium difficile to take over as a harmful pathogen to the colon after these good bacteria are killed. These "good" bacteria are often destroyed after treating an infection somewhere in the body with an antibiotic. The stronger, more complex antibiotic often leads to destruction of more of these good bacteria.

The rectum receives the stool from the colon. Due to the nerve innervation within the rectum, it sends a message to our brain reminding us that there is stool present to be evacuated. Once that message is received, an attempt can be made to evacuate the stool. The brain sets in motion impulses to the rectal area that results in the rectal sphincter relaxing and the rectal wall contracting. This provides the needed help to expel the stool.

The last part of the tract is the anus. It has muscles that connect to the pelvic floor area and the internal and external anal sphincters. These muscles are arranged in a way that it forms an angle or shelflike area, preventing the stool from exiting until engaging the defecation process. The anal sphincters work in tandem to prevent or release stool at the appropriate time.

Oh, the Things That Could Go Wrong!

Since discussion of our "bowel function" is not a hot topic at parties, I have taken a little more time in this chapter to discuss more of the multiple step-by-step processes required just to transport our food from one end of the digestive system to the other. I did not enter into a discussion about how carbohydrates in our food break down into sugars or the biochemical reactions required for bile to reduce fat in our diet or how these absorbed fats can increase our triglycerides and put us at risk of developing pancreatitis or how high-cholesterol foods put us at risk for heart attacks. Malfunction in any part of the forty-five-or-so feet of the gastrointestinal system can produce anything from minor annoyances to catastrophic events. There are some internal and external factors that can affect the intestines that we may not recognize. Stress, anxiety, and depression can produce stimulation of the brain and nervous system that can have an effect on the digestive system. These stimulations can produce symptoms such as abdominal cramps, diarrhea, and constipation. The gastrointestinal system and the brain are interconnected by the transport of nerve impulses back and forth. Eating habits that change when you are stressed can also affect how the bowel functions. Lastly, a "well-balanced meal" can be helpful in providing a more consistent bowel function. Lists differ as to what is included in a well-balanced meal. In general, it includes fresh fruits, fresh vegetables, whole grains, legumes, nuts, and lean proteins. Our ancient ancestors were more likely to have eaten this kind of diet. Since that time, the invention of foods that provide "empty calories" such as cookies, donuts, sodas, processed meats, and the like have made it more difficult to stay within the lines.

Contrary to some of the other organs or organ systems, the gastrointestinal system will remind you that it is present several times each week. As you go through this week, think about the foods you eat and how they are converted into energy, new muscle fibers, new skin formation, and new hair. If you are fortunate to have food readily available in your community, think of what a blessing that is. Think about the preparation of the foods before they reach the grocery stores and how you prepare them at home in order to make them safe. Then look at some verses in the book of Leviticus (next page), and read about the amazing instructions that God gave the Hebrew people on how to avoid getting sick by choosing the right food to eat. For example, God instructed the Hebrew people to avoid eating pig or pork (it was not an animal that chewed the cud). Pig meat often contained a type of roundworm that causes an infection known as trichinosis. This infection was acquired by eating the parasitic larva from raw or undercooked pig meat. Now that food preparation is different, and our cooking knowledge and technique is improved, this infection is infrequent.

Think about why your mouth waters when you smell or see food. Think about how people who make commercials use this information to trigger that response in you. Consider why wonderful food images appear when you get hungry. There is a strong communication between the brain and the gastrointestinal tract.

Consider how the gastrointestinal system is an irreducibly complex system. Without the liver and the pancreas, it would not function normally. Imagine something like hydrochloric acid that is strong enough to burn the skin yet is harmless to the stomach.

Biblical References to the Digestive System

Bowel and intestine are referred to in the Bible some five times. The most interesting biblical verses referring to the digestive system are found in Leviticus chapter 11 as clean versus unclean foods are discussed. God addressed these foods because of the beneficial or potential harmful effects they would have of the digestive system and the people's health. Here are some examples:

Bowel or intestine

- 2 Chronicles 21:12–19: Because Jehoram "did evil in the eyes of the Lord" (v. 6), "Elijah the prophet said, 'You yourself will be very ill with a lingering disease of the *bowels,* until the disease causes your *bowels* to come out'… In the course of time, at the end of the second year, his *bowels* came out because of the disease, and he died in great pain." It is thought that Jehoram had rectal cancer.
- Acts 1:18: "With the payment he received for his wickedness, Judas bought a field; there he fell headlong, his body burst open and all his *intestines* spilled out."

What foods to eat and what foods to avoid in Leviticus 11

As I mentioned at the end of chapter 6, you might say that Leviticus reveals guides that God gave which are similar to what would be given by our current-day county health departments. These instructions to prevent spread of disease by cautious food choices occurred thousands of years before the discovery of parasites, bacteria, and the like.

I will try to summarize parts of Leviticus chapter 11 by listing "clean foods" (those that were to be eaten) and "unclean foods" (those that were not to be eaten).

Clean Foods (Eat)	Unclean Foods (Avoid Eating)
animals—split hoof / chews cud	missing one or both (split hoof / chews cud)
fish—fins and scales	missing one or both (fins or scales)
birds—non-scavengers/ non-predators	scavengers/predators
ground—locusts, grass-hopper, crickets	reptiles/rodents

Why did God warn his people about the categories of some food? Let's look at a few of them:

- Pig (disapproved to eat): Pigs in the wild are scavengers that eat almost anything including garbage, rodents, and rotting carcasses. They do not chew their cud, which means that they don't have an extra stomach that can hold the food after chewing it, and then regurgitate it back up to chew it again. The cow is an animal that "chews its cud." You will often see them just standing in a pasture and chewing and chewing and chewing. That helps to cleanse the food of bacteria it has eaten. The pig only digests their food in total for four hours, which does not clear toxins from their system and meats.
- Cow (approved to eat): Chews its cud (regurgitates food from first stomach back into the mouth) and digests food thoroughly. Clears the toxins.

- Catfish (disapproved to eat along with oysters, shrimp, squid): Because they are bottom dwellers, they ingest toxic materials from riverbeds. They are a source of hepatitis A and Vibrio bacteria. This was more prominent prior to developing adequate human waste management.
- Crappie (approved to eat): They are not bottom dwellers. They have fins and scales.
- Vulture (disapproved to eat): Scavengers/predator. They kill and eat other animals including the dead and putre-fying flesh. They eat items that would make humans sick should they eat them.
- Duck (approved to eat): They eat grain and stay away from the food of vultures.

Because God wanted his chosen people to be healthy and reflect on who he was, he instructed them with amazing information that was some 3,500 years ahead of science!

Two Questions about the Digestive System

First question: What about the digestive system makes me think that divine creation was involved?

Second question: What about the digestive system makes me think that it developed by chance?

Below, jot down characteristics that would support both options.

Divine Design?	Developed by Chance?

CHAPTER 8

THE BRAIN

Four facts about the brain:

1. The brain consists of one hundred to two hundred billion nerves or neurons. Brain tissue the size of a grain of sand can contain one hundred thousand neurons.
2. The brain reaches its maturity at approximately age 25.
3. Your thoughts today are similar to 90 percent of your previous day's thoughts.
4. Sleep is imperative for proper brain functioning.

The brain is the most complex part of the body. Based on its complexity, of all the organs in the human body, it is probably the least completely understood. It is similar to the central processing unit within a computer. I say similar because despite how complex the most sophisticated computer is, the brain is multiple times more complex. It is the part of the body in which multiple functions of the body are controlled and executed. It controls all of our voluntary and involuntary movements and bodily functions. It interconnects and communicates with each part of the body through the nervous system. As we have seen in the previous chapters, the nervous system innervates all of our other organs in order for them to function properly and maintain a healthy existence.

The nervous system consists of the brain, the spinal cord, and nerves. The brain receives information from your eyes, ears, nose and other sensory organs. It then processes this information and generates ideas and thoughts that eventually lead to actions in other parts of the body.

The brain sends messages to the body through the spinal cord and nerves. This can lead to production of movement through muscle contraction and relaxation, speech, and other activity as it affects muscles and other organs and organ systems to act based on the input to them. The brain also has centers within it that control body functions without having to think about them such as your heart rate, breathing, and blood pressure.

When you look at the brain (see image 9), it might appear that there are two brains. However, the two major cerebral hemispheres of the brain are connected and communicate with each other through a thick band of tissue known as the corpus callosum.

Different parts of the brain control different functions of the body as well as which hand becomes our dominant, or go-to hand. About 90 percent of the people are right-hand dominant. They use their right hand more frequently to do certain tasks such as eat, dribble a ball, or write. The other 10 percent are mostly left-hand dominant although there is a small group of people who can use both hands equally well and are known as ambidextrous. There are different theories as to why this is the case.

The right side of the brain controls muscles on the left side of the body, and the left side of the brain controls muscles on the right side of the body. In general, sensory impulses from the left side of the body cross to the right brain and vice versa. Therefore, damage to one side of the brain will affect the opposite side of the body's motor and sensory functions.

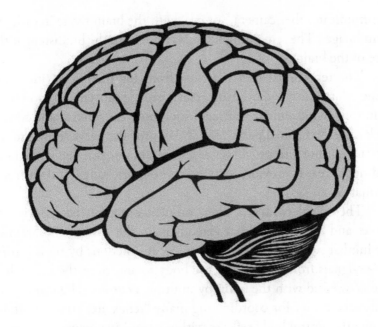

Image 9: Brain (Side View)

Amazingly, in about 95 percent of the right-handed people, the left side of the brain is dominant for developing language skills. Also, in about 60–75 percent of the left-handed people, language is developed in the left side of the brain. The left hemisphere of the brain is also dominant for understanding math and logic. The right hemisphere is helpful in understanding spatial thoughts, music, and visual imagery. So, if you are more analytical and methodical in your thinking, you are probably using more left-brain neurons. If you are more creative and artistic, you tend to exercise the neurons on the right side. The world is a more interesting place because some people are more gifted on one side of the brain or the other.

The brain and the spinal cord have multiple nerves that exit to various parts of the body. The brain provides twelve pairs of nerves that emerge directly from the brain including the brainstem. These "cranial" nerves mainly affect the face, the neck, and the sensory organs of the head. Cranial nerve I (CN I) affects the sense of smell in the nose while cranial nerve 2 (CN II) is called the optic nerve and communicates the "camera," or eye, with the brain tissue in order to form images. The remaining ten CNs arise from the brainstem at the base of the brain.

The ten cranial nerves arising from the brainstem, innervate tissue related to eye movement, facial muscle movement and sensation, tongue movement and sensation, inner ear activity, and several neck muscles. Cranial nerve 10 (CN10) provides nerve stimuli to the external ear but also provides nerve stimuli to organs below the head and neck area. It provides activity to the heart, lungs, and gastrointestinal tract.

The spinal cord is a long, tubular structure that consists of nerves and nerve tissue that extends from the base of the brain to the lumbar region of the skeletal spine. It functions by transmitting nerve signals from all parts of the body to and from the brain. It is interconnected with the brain by multiple neurons. The spinal cord is also the center for coordinating many "reflex arcs" that can independently control body reflexes without requiring neuron activity to even reach the brain. The spinal cord is about eighteen inches long. It is protected by the skeletal system's vertebra.

The brain and the spinal cord make up the central nervous system (CNS). (See image 10.) All the nerves that branch out from the brain and spinal cord and extend to other parts of the body, including our muscles and organs, are known as the peripheral nervous system. The nerves that exit the spinal cord are categorized into four segments. The cervical (neck) area sends nerves to primarily the shoulders, arms, hands, and upper body. The thoracic (main torso) area sends nerves to the chest, abdomen, and torso. The lumbar (lower back) area sends nerves to the legs, feet, and toes. The sacral (pelvic) area sends nerves to the pelvic and buttock regions.

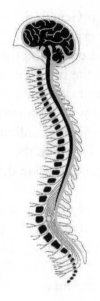

Image 10: Brain and Spinal Cord (Side View), Spinal
Cord—Peripheral Nerves Origin (Frontal View)

As you look at the spinal cord, you can see why a severe accident could cause someone to be a paraplegic if their spinal cord is severed at a level above where the leg and feet nerves exit the spinal canal. This would eliminate nerve innervation and function to those muscles and other organs. You would see muscle wasting, or deterioration, in those muscles because nerve stimulation is imperative for the muscle function and maintenance. If the spinal cord was severed in the upper cervical region, quadriplegia would result.

Wait! What Makes the Brain Work?

The supernatural question about the central nervous system and other parts of the human body such as the physical heart (remember the heart's pacemaker) is what triggers, or "fires," these organs to begin and continue their functions in the first place? Not *how* do they work but *what* initiates and makes them continue to work? Could the answer to *what* makes organs such as the brain and heart

75

continue to function on their own be found in Genesis 2:7 or Job 32:8? As a physician, I have not found a better explanation.

Scientists have tried for years, with some success, to explain how the brain functions. They have looked at how the brain forms and gathers data from the environment in order to help formulate the choices we make. They have outlined nerve pathways from the brain to muscles and skin sensory areas, making it easier for medical providers to diagnose and treat certain conditions. However, the answer as to where within the human body do choice and decision develop remains elusive to the scientific community.

Remember back in chapter 4 as we discussed the human heart, I quoted Dallas Willard's thoughts about this nonmuscle "second heart" that dwells within each human. Here is that quote:

> Heart refers to its position in the human being, as the center or core to which every other component of the self owes its proper functioning.

He goes on to say,

> The human heart, will, or spirit is the executive center of a human life. The heart is where decisions and choices are made for the whole person.

Where is this second heart located within the body, you might ask? Were we able to locate this heart while doing our cadaver dissections in the lab?

One of my favorite authors, Tim Keller (with Kathy Keller), summarizes the problem of not seeing the human being as a spirit-guided creation this way:

> We can't fix human problems with mere technology and knowledge... Science can't change the heart. We may study racism, crime, and poverty and make some advances. But the

view that every phenomenon has a natural cause
and therefore a technological solution in the
end fails because this simply isn't true. There are
supernatural, spiritual problems that need supernatural, spiritual remedies. In the end, the more
we know the more we see how little we know...
Human reason unaided by God's revelation will
never give us the whole picture.[11]

Understanding God's revelation about how all of creation works
as well as how we form or reform our spirit because of this revelation
will aid us in the choices and decisions that we make. Those choices
and decisions will aid us in formulating solutions for many of our
difficult problems. Science, by itself, cannot arrive at the same decisions because it is only dealing with human matter. There is nothing
within the scientific realm that can change the way that the spirit
functions.

As we entertain more thoughts about this supernatural state,
think back to the problems with Darwin's theory that we discussed
in chapter 2. Not only was Darwin hampered by the fact that he was
not able to see the functions within the cell nor uncover other "black
boxes," his theory was also hampered by attempting to find a physical
or natural cause for everything. No amount of human observation or
examining the structure of the brain itself can explain the diversity
of thought and decision-making that is seen from person to person.

Just as we don't understand "how" our thoughts and ideas
always originate, there is a supernatural aspect to the executive center
that controls how we arrive at our choices, ideas, and understanding
of human life. The brain feeds information into that executive center
known as our heart, or as I prefer to use the word, spirit. Most people define the spirit as the nonphysical part of a person which is the
center or seat of emotions and character. Thoughts and ideas develop
or are triggered within the brain from books we read, our environment, and other forms of input from the body such as from the eyes,
ears, skin, tongue, and nose. However, regardless of the images and
thoughts that originate in our brain, they are controlled by the exec-

utive center known as our spirit. Our spirit makes a decision to react or not react in certain ways based on our perception of the input and how our human spirit has been formed.

For example, two people may be walking toward the doors of a concert. Both of them hear shots ring out from inside the building where the concert is held. The same sensory information is recorded in each person's brain. However, one person's spirit leads him through the doors in order to help overcome the situation, while the other person's spirit leads him in the other direction far away from the event.

What causes this dichotomy of choice between two different people? I do not pretend to know all of the cause-and-effect relationships that our spirit uses to make every choice in life. However, if the brain's input is identical, but is controlled differently by two different individuals, in a physically unseen part of our human existence, the choices and decisions that are made by those two individuals are evidence that this component of the human being does actually exist.

As you work through this book, I think you will see how the body is one of those things mentioned in Romans chapter 1 that can be seen with our own eyes and reveals the necessity of a creator. When investigating the visualized parts of the body, you do not have to begin with a preconceived idea about the existence of God. However, because of the body's amazing consistency, millions of reproducible biochemical reactions, interdependent organ functions, and its core executive center from which choice and decisions are made, I believe you will see that there is no other explanation. What I learned in medical school because of unexplained aspects of the human body led me to investigate what these other components were and how they were involved in our lives.

To highlight a few of the unexplained characteristics discovered in medical school and mentioned earlier, consider these: What makes the physical (muscle) heart beat for eighty years on its own without some outside source to trigger the initiation of each beat? How can millions of biochemical reactions occur minute by minute within the body with absolute precision and consistency? The third—and one of the most interesting of these unexplained aspects or functions of the human body—is what triggers thoughts and ideas to be formed within our brain without any apparent input from an outside source such as one of the senses? What causes these thoughts and ideas to be different, depending on whether we are under stress, relaxed, angry, or depressed? Why are some thoughts and ideas "parked" in the brain only to resurface at a later time? Why do more complex decisions form in this executive center due to repetitively visiting certain thoughts and ideas?

Another thing to consider is, what causes the same formed images within different people's brains to be processed differently. Those produced images often lead to thoughts and ideas within our brain. Those produced thoughts and ideas then often lead to choices or decisions. There must exist another level other than the brain to provide a processing center for those thoughts and ideas in order to arrive at choices and decisions. You might say, "Well, the brain is what produces the choice or decision." If that was the case, based on just the physical structure of the brain, would not the brain of one individual also produce the same or very similar choices and decisions that someone else's brain would make with the identical input? If you look at any function of the human body, it is almost identical to the next person's compared body function. If you have a burn on the arm, does it not heal in almost the identical same way for each individual? If two individuals look upon the same object, do their brains not form the same image.? If my friend and I both are looking at a dog, does one of us see a dog and the other see a cat?

Yet the same input entering into the brain of two different individuals can lead to a decision point that is totally opposite from one another. There is a thought evaluation and processing center within each of us that leads to those different choices and decisions. Those choices and decisions are dependent upon how this center is formed within an individual. I believe this processing center is malleable and is known as the human spirit.

According to Ecclesiastes 3:11, this human spirit is located within each created human being. (The term *human spirit* should be differentiated from the term *Holy Spirit* or just *Spirit* with a capital S. The Holy Spirit is that part of the Trinity that is gifted to dwell within those who become a disciple of Jesus. The Holy Spirit is an additional layer of help and comfort to our God-given spirit which is given to each of us at our creation.) This eternal spirit component operates within each of us and connects us to our creator. That is the component that is the source of many of our decisions that can provide an avenue to a happy and healthier existence.

Certainly, all our formed thoughts and ideas do not originate from God. It seems apparent that many other thoughts that originate from outside stimuli come into the brain and are sent to the spirit for decision-making or choice. The spirit receives "good" input from the experiences of our mind, body, and nature. It also receives "bad" input from the experiences of our mind, body, and nature. Our spirit is formed from how we process and decide to deal with this input.

Oscar Wilde said, "By age 40, we have the face that we deserve." It depends on how God's guidance from his owner's manual has been followed as to what has molded and shaped that face that we display to others. That face may be one of joy, or it may be one of anguish. What input forms this spirit within us determines how our countenance forms and how we display that important part of us.

Some of today's medical schools have recognized the importance of teaching the spiritual heart aspect of the human. They are teaching this not just for the sake of information but for the purpose of formation or transformation. This teaching is an attempt to understand how the "whole" body functions and how this leads to our opportunity to live out the healthiest existence possible here on earth.

This week, think about why you think about the things you think about. (Sort of a tongue twister, isn't it?) Think about what causes thoughts in your brain to suddenly appear without any apparent outside stimuli. Since we are not robots, consider how our brain takes an image, thought, or idea and turns it into an action, a choice, or a decision. Contemplate about your brain's infinite storage capacity. Why, if the brain's capacity to learn is virtually unlimited, do you have trouble memorizing the five steps to resolving a math problem? Can we truly think about two things at once? Look at your hand or your foot and think about how amazing it is to be able to move it by just thinking about that process. Even more amazing, consider your ability to move it without even thinking about the process as you go to open the refrigerator door while you are contemplating what you are going to eat. Finally, try to find evidence or develop a logical theory that would explain how or where decisions and choices are made other than within the human spirit.

Some of these ideas will be discussed further in the conclusion and in Appendix A.

Biblical References to the Brain

The actual word *brain* is not used in the Bible, but the words *thought(s)* and *idea(s)* are used some 143 times. Here are some examples:

- Genesis 6:5: "The Lord saw how great the wickedness of the human race had become on the earth, and that every inclination of the *thoughts* of the human heart was only evil all the time." Our thoughts are processed through the filter of the human heart or spirit.
- 1 Samuel 27:1: "But David *thought* to himself…"
- Psalm 55:2: "My *thoughts* trouble me and I am distraught." Our thoughts and ideas can trouble us in many ways. Sometimes they produce physical symptoms such as headaches, diarrhea, or palpitations (feeling of your heartbeat).
- Psalm 139:2: "You know when I sit and when I rise; you perceive my *thoughts* from afar." It is hard to understand how our creator can be all knowing.
- Ecclesiastes 2:12: "Then I turned my *thoughts* to consider wisdom, and also madness and folly." Our thoughts sometimes are all over the place.
- Matthew 9:4: Knowing their thoughts, Jesus said, "Why do you entertain evil *thoughts* in your hearts."
- Matthew 15:19: "For out of the heart come evil *thoughts*." Just as good thoughts come from the heart, so can evil ones. The thoughts go from the brain to our heart (spirit)

to process and then thoughts are formed within the heart (spirit) and sent back with different formed ideas which may be healthy or unhealthy.

- John 18:34: In response to Pilate asking Jesus if he was the king of the Jews, Jesus asked, "is that your own *idea*...or did others talk to you about me?"
- Acts 17:20: "You are bringing some strange *ideas* to our ears, and we would like to know what they mean." Thoughts and ideas can be different before and after they are processed by our spirit.
- 1 Timothy 6:20: "Turn away from godless chatter and the opposing *ideas* of what is falsely called knowledge."

Discerning true from false knowledge is something our spirit assists us in. Discernment is much needed in our society today.

For examples of Bible verses that refer to the heart (spirit, will, or choice), see Appendix A.

Two Questions about the Brain

First question: What about the brain makes me think that divine creation was involved?

Second question: What about the brain makes me think that it developed by chance?

Below, jot down characteristics that would support both options.

DIVINE DESIGN?   DEVELOPED BY CHANCE?

CHAPTER 9

THE MIRACLE

Wikipedia (Oxford/Lexico) defines a miracle as "a supernatural event that seems inexplicable by natural or scientific laws." Some recorded biblical examples of a miracle might be the resurrection from the dead, parting of the Red Sea, and manna and quail from heaven. There is a human event that most consider to be more natural than miraculous that I consider to be the latter. It is an event to which every human being has been exposed, one that "seems inexplicable by natural and scientific laws," one that has thousands of chances to go awry but rarely does, one that involves changes within the organs that we have discussed to this point in the book. That "miracle" is the pregnancy and birth process.

Pregnancy and childbirth are unique events revealing the miracle and power of nature and its creator. As a family physician, I directed the medical care of pregnant patients and delivered babies. It was during this time that I experienced some of the most fascinating structural and biochemical events that occur within the human body. The process known as gestation, with its multiple steps, culminates in the delivery of this miraculous bundle known as a baby. If these amazing steps are not enough, shortly after birth, a child is disconnected from the life-giving nutrients of the mother by clamping and cutting the umbilical cord. This forces another set of events to occur that allows the child to live in a more independent environment with help from others by way of an alternative nourishment and protection plan.

The pregnancy and birth processes would appear to be somewhat routine because it occurs worldwide some 350,000 times daily. In only a very small sample of cases does it occur with any devastating results. However, this process is anything but routine. The miracle is in the events that transpire from development of a single fertilized cell to a mature newborn and in the revealed changes in the woman's body to prepare for pregnancy and delivery. Trying to calculate the possibilities of the exact makeup of a newborn is beyond mathematical comprehension. In other words, it is more likely for you to win the Mega Millions jackpot lottery (1 in 292.2 million) multiple times than it is for the you to map out all of the sequence possibilities in the development and birth of a child. Yet despite these many differing patterns and sequences that occur, the human continues to produce one after the other with the same precise biochemical reactions, organ system functions, and general anatomy. Let's look at some of these amazing structural and biochemical events.

The body is made up of 30 to 100 trillion cells. To give you a number comparison to think about, the national debt as of July 2020 was approximately $25 trillion dollars. What occurs that leads to these thirty to one hundred trillion cells? Why do some cells perform certain functions and others do not? Why do we all look different (except for identical twins which we will discuss later)? Why is the human birth process more dangerous than other mammals? The answers to all these questions lie in the multiple complex sequences that happen over a nine-month period that produces possibilities that are indeed mathematically incomprehensible.

As most adults know, the creation of a newborn begins with the contact of a sperm with an egg. Before that can occur, these cells have to be produced and placed into a position that is conducive for their success to connect and become one.

Sperm are produced in the testicle as puberty in the male begins. The testicle is made up of tiny tubules that if stretched out would be approximately one mile long. A male produces approximately one hundred million new sperm each day. Each sperm carries a unique genetic package. Each cell of the body, including sperm, contain forty-six chromosomes of which two are sex chromosomes. The male has a X and a Y sex chromosome, and a female has two X sex chromosomes. Each chromosome has hundreds to thousands of genes. This makes for about thirty thousand genes per cell. Because of the DNA chance sequences, each sperm carries genetic makeup never found before.

Unlike the male, who begins producing sperm around puberty, the female has the largest number of eggs when she is in the fetus stage in utero (about two months into the nine-month cycle of pregnancy). In the fetus stage, she has approximately six million eggs, and they start to die or diminish from that time forward. At birth, the female has about one to two million eggs left; at age 30, 70,000 to 100,000 eggs; at age forty, 18,000 to 20,000 eggs. Usually, one egg in the ovary is released each month during a small window of time that is controlled by the woman's hormones and biochemical changes. This is known as ovulation. That release from the ovary occurs near the distal end of the fallopian tube then enters the tube, where it parks, ready to connect with a sperm. (See image 11.)

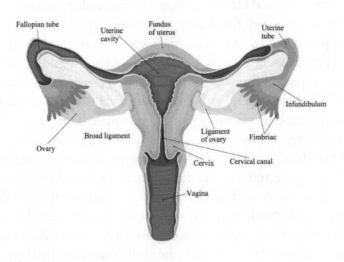

Image 11: The Female Reproductive System

It would appear that all that needs to take place at this point is to send in a sperm and "voila." However, not one but three hundred million sperm are sent toward the cervix at each sexual encounter. The chances of one of these sperm becoming successful in penetrating the egg is dependent and controlled by the woman's body. During days surrounding ovulation, the woman's body experiences biochemical reactions which cause the cervical mucus to become thinner, which allows sperm to enter and travel down the fallopian tube. At this point, the sperm is about six inches away from the egg. This requires about a two-day swim from that point in the tube to reach the egg. Even when it reaches the egg, the egg has a number of support cells around it and is particular about which sperm gets in. The overwhelming number of sperm are rejected for different reasons. The selected sperm then sheds an outer coating and forces its way into the egg. The cell membranes and the chromosomes of the egg and the sperm combine the DNA of the cells which is followed by the first cell division usually within twenty-four hours. Then the cells divide more rapidly. Occasionally, after combining their DNA, the tiny cell will split into two cells that each contain identical DNA and, hence, produce identical twins. Both would be male or both female. Fraternal twins occur when more than one egg is fertilized by more than one sperm. Fraternal twins can both be girls, both boys, or a mix of a girl and a boy. Each would have different DNA sequences. Because the mathematical possibilities are incomprehensible, there have never been two identical people with identical genetic makeup born via two separate pregnancies. This is also true for two separate egg-sperm fertilizations in the same pregnancy.

After the egg is fertilized by the sperm, it starts its trip down the fallopian tube and into the uterus where it burrows into the uterine lining on the sixth day. At two weeks, it forms into an embryo. At three weeks, the neural tube and brain begin to form. The heart begins to beat at four weeks. At thirty-two days, the arms and hands begin developing. At two months from the time that the sperm fertilizes the egg, the tissue is known as a fetus. At that time, it is about one to one-half inches long and weighs about one-third ounce.

During the fourth to twelfth week of gestation, the embryo/fetus undergoes rapid cell division and growth. If it continued that same rate of growth throughout the remaining pregnancy period, the newborn would weigh one to one and a half tons. Needless to say, it is a good thing that the growth process begins to decelerate.

About this time, the nutrients needed for growth are going to the fetus via the placenta, and the umbilical cord attached to the uterus. The placenta is of dual origin, comprising both fetal and maternal elements. All the necessary fluids and oxygen are being provided to the baby through it. If a fetus is in need of a vitamin or iron, it will steal if from the mother at the expense of the mother being deplete in that ingredient.

The miracle of the pregnancy process also lies in the activity of the DNA that make up the genes and chromosome material. As mentioned before, each cell has forty-six chromosomes and approximately thirty thousand genes. Not all cells in the body behave the same. Different cells perform different functions. Some genes during the formation of the baby are turned on, and some are turned off during the uterine process. This allows for the differentiation of parts of the body like the arms and legs, the eyes, bone, and the heart. How do cells turn on the right genes? Part of the miracle of a baby's development is the fact that certain biochemical messages are sent to turn these genes on, and then later, biochemical messages are sent that turn these genes off. This produces arms and legs that are equal in length and size. This allows for different facial features to develop (although those of us with big ears might wish the genes had been turned off a little earlier).

Most believe that during the first half of the gestational period (first twenty weeks), the gonads and tubes in the fetus can become ovaries and fallopian tubes or testicles and spermatic tubes, depending on what genes are turned on in the fetus during the process. There is also a period of time when genes apparently send messages to some tissue that cause the cells to stop producing and die. For instance, the weblike tissue between the fingers noted on early ultrasounds resolves because of this process. If that did not happen and the tissue continued to grow, we would be born with webbed hands.

Eventually, at about nine months, it is time for the birth process to occur. Human births are more dangerous and painful than other mammals. This is in part due to the brain being larger in humans and the mom's pelvic structure smaller. It is also partly due to the creation of humans to walk in a more upright position (Genesis 3:16 may have a little to do with it also). The baby must go through numerous contortions to make it through the birth canal including overlapping of several bones that make up the cranium or head. This can occur because these bones are in segments and not fully connected until several months after birth.

Cutting the Cord

There is an analogy used at times when referring to a child that has become an adult who does not want to leave home. Someone may say, "It's time to cut the cord." This means that it is time for that adult to leave the dependency of the parent and to become independent on his or her own. When it is time for that process to occur in the newborn, the baby's cord is cut, and certain changes begin to occur that will lead to the independent life of the newborn. The placenta to which the cord is attached has provided nutrition and helped the baby "breathe" while in the uterus. It has been the source of oxygen during the pregnancy. Shortly after birth, the cord is clamped and cut, and the baby takes its first breath. At that time, the blood flow to the lungs decreases, the fluid that was in the lungs drains or is absorbed from the lungs, and the lungs inflate. They begin the process of working independently to provide oxygen to the blood on inspiration and remove carbon dioxide on expiration.

With the inflation of the lungs and the clamping of the cord, the blood flow to the lung blood vessels increases, which is necessary for those vessels to be exposed to the now-aerated lungs in order to transport oxygen to all parts of the infant. Two openings in and around the heart that were necessary in the fetal circulation, the foramen ovale and the ductus arteriosus, close, eventually producing an adult pattern of blood flow into the heart and lungs. This transition from total support of the baby by mom to an independent existence for the infant occurs in short order.

Shortly after birth, changes in the mother's body are occurring also. The placenta is released and delivered. The hormone oxytocin, which had been stored earlier in pregnancy to prevent premature delivery and was released during labor to trigger contractions, is now responsible for continued contractions of the uterus to help decrease bleeding. After birth, the skin-to-skin contact of the baby and the mother may increase the production of oxytocin as well.

Shortly after giving birth, estrogen and progesterone hormone levels decrease, and the level of prolactin increases. This hormone shift gives way for breasts to begin forming breastmilk for the baby's consumption. This increase in blood flow and milk production to the breasts lead to the breast becoming full and is known as breast engorgement. As the child is nursed or other non-nursing steps are taken, this engorgement resolves.

Multiple other changes occur within the mom's body that I will not cover here but can be researched by looking up postpartum changes in the mother.

Biblical References to Pregnancy and Birth

There are multiple references to the pregnancy and the birth process in the Bible. *Pregnancy* is listed 40 times, *born* 174, *birth* 143, and *womb* 63. Here are a few examples:

- Genesis 4:1: "Adam made love to his wife Eve and she became *pregnant* and gave *birth* to Cain." The first mention of *sex, pregnancy*, and *delivery* in the Bible.
- Genesis 3:16: "To the woman he said, 'I will make your pains in *childbearing* very severe.'" For her part in the disobedience of God, labor and childbirth was to be a painful experience going forward.
- Job 1:21: "Naked I came from my mother's *womb*, and naked I will depart." This was Job's reply to having lost his sons and daughters. This is a truism for all of us.
- Psalm 139:13: "For you created my inmost being; you knit me together in my mother's *womb*." A reference to our Creator's knowledge of each of us and his miraculous process known as fetal development.
- Hebrews 11:11: "And by faith, even Sarah, who was past *childbearing* age, was enabled to bear children because she

considered him faithful who had made the promise." Sarah
delivered Isaac at the ripe old age of ninety. This, even at
that time, was considered a double miracle as Sarah was
considered past childbearing age.

- Luke 2:11: "Today in the town of David, a Savior has been
  born to you: he is the Messiah, the Lord." The recorded
  birth of the incarnate son of God, Jesus, in a manger.

- Jeremiah 1:5: "Before I formed you in the *womb* I knew
  you, before you were born, I set you apart; I appointed
  you as a prophet to the nations." Another word for *knew*
  is "chose." It is a little hard for us as humans to think that
  we can be chosen and predestined to be conformed to the
  image of Jesus yet have full choice within the framework of
  how God made us.

- Ecclesiastes 3:1–2: "There is a time for everything, and a
  season for every activity under the heavens: a time to be
  born and a time to die." Life continues here on earth (under
  the sun, 1:9) and according to Solomon is meaningless
  without the respect for God and his instruction for our
  lives (12:13).

Two Questions about Pregnancy and Childbirth

First question: What about pregnancy and childbirth make me
think that divine creation was involved?

Second question: What about pregnancy and childbirth make
me think that it developed by chance?

Below, jot down characteristics that would support both options.

DIVINE DESIGN? | DEVELOPED BY CHANCE?

C O N C L U S I O N

THE GUM WRAPPER

Have you every performed the simple task of bending down and picking up a gum wrapper that you accidentally dropped near a busy street? Simple, right? Let's go through just a few of the steps that must transpire in order for this seemingly simple task to occur.

First, the sense of touch is engaged by the nerves located in the skin for you to realize that you have dropped something. The brain tells you that it is no longer grasped by your fingers. Your conscience, or thoughts and decisions, are engaged to suggest that you probably should pick it up and not litter. The eyes move to locate the wrapper so that you can start the process of retrieving it. Both eyes move in the exact same direction so as not to produce double or blurred vision. After the muscles in the neck are engaged to turn the head in the direction of the wrapper, the brain processes the camera image of the wrapper, and your spirit makes a decision as to whether it is safe to pick up the wrapper. You would not want to pick it up if the wind blew it into oncoming traffic.

If the brain confirms that it is safe, it sends a message to the legs to start to move in that direction. The nerves that connect the muscles to the central nervous system via the peripheral nervous system are engaged so that the muscles attached to the skeleton move the body in that direction, all the time staying in focus with the eyes by moving the six muscles in each eye in unison so a clear picture is maintained. Once the legs move your body near the wrapper, the brain processes the distance that you have to bend in order to pick it up. You don't want to overshoot and fall on your face. Your distance is calculated, and the brain then sends impulses into the midbody muscles to start their movement in order to bend. The brain, which has already calculated the distance that you need to bend, engages your arms to start to reach toward the wrapper.

At this time, the body adjusts your blood pressure slightly to avoid passing out as you bend over. As you bend over, the midbody muscles and legs shift slightly to force the buttock area backward so you can maintain your balance. The entire time this is happening, the anal sphincter and bladder sphincter (muscle) are maintaining good control so that you don't have an "accident" or feel the urgency to go to the bathroom before you retrieve the paper. The heart rate may slightly increase to control the blood pressure, which provides blood to the brain in order for the brain to retrieve oxygen. The brain is controlling and often suppressing most all other thoughts in order to finish this task. As the arms are reaching for the wrapper, the brain controls the thumb, index, and middle finger of your dominant hand to start to grasp the wrapper.

The sense of touch in the skin lets you know when the wrapper is contacted, and the wrapper is grasped by the aforementioned digits. At this point, the eyes send a message to the brain that we have the wrapper. The brain then goes through the exact reverse order of thoughts (I'll spare you those) that transpired in the above sequence in order to stand erect. Then the spirit makes a decision to either put the wrapper in your pocket or purse or look for a trash can to dispose of it. If you put it in your pocket or purse, you have completed your task. If, however, you decide to place it in a trash can, there is more work to do. I will spare you of those steps as well.

Whew. All that just to pick up a wrapper and dispose of it? I wanted to discuss some of the steps required to pick up a gum wrapper so that we can appreciate how the body is so interconnected and dependent on its many parts to function as a whole. There are actually many steps that I left out in my description. Now, think about the required sequence of steps you would need to follow if you were performing a more sophisticated task such as that of piloting a plane, playing a Mozart piece of music, or working on a rapid-paced assembly line. Many tasks we do each day require more steps for the body than picking up a gum wrapper.

Without the brain, the eye is only a camera. Without the peripheral nerves, the muscles waste away and don't work. Without the skin sending a message to the brain and muscle, the hand is not able to grasp anything. Without the body's regulation of blood pressure, you may pass out when you bend over. Without the six muscles moving the eye in unison, the paper would be blurred and cause you to overreach the wrapper when trying to pick it up. Without the brain controlling all these functions, nothing would get done.

I have not even attempted to discuss all the biochemical reactions and by-products that take place when putting the body in motion. There are literally millions of chemical reactions that are taking place in the body at any one time. The Kreb's cycle that was mentioned earlier is a series of chemical reactions that releases stored energy derived from carbohydrates, fats, and proteins from the foods we eat. The formation of ATP occurs to provide energy to drive the cell. Amino acids form into proteins to help build and maintain muscle and other tissue. The cells in our body use glucose, which breaks down during cellular respiration to release energy. The body uses enzymes which speed up the biochemical process in order to reduce the amount of energy needed to carry out a reaction.

I hope that you can agree with me that the body is an amazing creation. I have very superficially scratched the surface of the many volumes of information that is available about the human body. It would take the total volume of this book to describe all of the physical, mental, and biochemical processes to simply pick up a gum wrapper. That, however, would be a very boring book.

I also have not discussed at any length in the book the skeletal system and the production of blood within the bone marrow, the muscles, and how the body's energy drives them, the lymphatic system which cleans up fluids as well as helps prevent infection, the endocrine system which secretes hormones which help to regulate processes in our body such as metabolism, growth, and reproduction, or the urinary system and how the kidneys reserve fluid when we dehydrate as well as provide an avenue to excrete some of the by-products from food or drugs. The list of wonders about the human body could go on and on. One aspect of the human body may be of greater interest to a person than a different one. If your area of interest was not satisfied by the information in this book, let me encourage you to go to your local library or to a trusted website such as WebMD to investigate that area.

Our Environment

Our environment is another component that plays a huge role in shaping who we become as a person. We are all shaped by different experiences. This molding of our physical, mental, and spiritual lives comes from many areas.

As a child, I loved playing little league baseball. I had great coaches such as John L. Neely and my dad, who made the sport fun. It was also made memorable by being around my best friend, Roger, and other friends who played the sport. During the summer, Roger, Bill, Brian, Jerry, Curtis, Herschel, Raymond, Mike, and others would converge on an acre lot beside our house to play baseball. Many of us just knew that we were going to be the next Mickey Mantle or Roger Maris. (If I had only saved their baseball cards instead of using them in the spokes of my bike!) On the acre lot, we constructed a baseball field consisting of a wire backstop, bases, and a dirt road that was our homerun marker. There were no corn fields on the other side of the road as in the movie *Field of Dreams*, no ghosts of baseball legends walking across the road to join us, but man, did we have fun and build relationships. Later, during my adult life, I had the opportunity to coach my son, Eric, in youth baseball and my daughter, Amy, in youth softball. During those times, we were able to share successes in the sport, our love for the game, learn life lessons, and build additional relationships in the process. I believe that these relational and emotional bonds continue to shape us as we proceed down the road toward our intended destiny.

Mental health is a key component to having overall good health. It starts by experiencing the touch and nourishment you receive from your family. As you mature, you go through the process of introducing yourself to others and over time building trust and belief in them that they have your back. There is a mental need for this trust and belief in others. The brain is a very complex organ that produces thoughts and feelings. When those thoughts and feelings are shared with others, it can lead to potential release of hormones which may even aid in reducing the pain that may be experienced when those thoughts and feelings are difficult to process.

Our Human Spirit (Heart) and Our Choices

We have discussed the spirit at some length in chapter 8. As important as physical and mental health is, I found that those patients who truly experienced a measure of spiritual health had a degree of peace and joy that led to a more complete overall healthy existence. Whether it was a patient or the family member of a patient dealing with cancer, a person with a traumatic injury from an accident, or someone who had lost a loved one, there were similar emotional benefits that seemed to exist. While they might experience the same initial stress that other patients would experience, those with an emotionally healthy God-driven spirit would most often come out the other side with better overall health and even increased longevity. I think that had to do with a spirit within them that did not escape from reality when faced with difficult events in their lives. Peter Scazzero offered this in his book, *Emotionally Healthy Spirituality*:

> There is no greater disaster in the spiritual
> life than to be immersed in unreality. In fact, the
> true spiritual life is not an escape from reality but
> an absolute commitment to it.[12]

I think that this ability to face reality with a healthy spirit is a good place from which to operate.

Spiritual health, like mental health, also requires relationship building. Introducing or reintroducing yourself to your Creator, observing the creation around you in order to build trust and belief in him, and practicing your connection with the creator in ways that your human spirit begins to discern a level of guidance for you, are all needed for you to be spiritually healthy. I know this seems supernatural, and a component of it is. The human spirit is the unseen and unmeasurable core of the human where choices are made during our daily lives. I believe that every human being has this Creator-gifted component known as the spirit that is actually living within them. From that standpoint, it is not supernatural. The spirit itself connects with us in various ways such as the nudge you get from your conscience when it is decision time. You may be considering two different decisions. The spirit may help to provide clarity in order for you to choose between those decisions. You can see the spirit's work within those who seem to be at peace even in the presence of losing a loved one. You see it as a perceived need to pray when you are facing a catastrophic event. You saw the spirit developed into a full extent in the compassioned life of the late Mother Teresa.

When I attended medical school, there was minimal attention given to this important aspect of our being. Medical school's task, at that time, was to teach us how the "seen" aspects of the body fit together nicely in order to provide a seamless human being. It also taught us what to do as physicians to help keep all the organs and organ systems maintaining that seamless function. However, the unexplainable things that seemed to evolve in my study in medical school led me to investigate this "unseen" inner core of the human.

This spiritual health is mainly experienced and nourished by your human spirit engaging with the Creator's Spirit. Think of someone with whom you would like to build a relationship and become their friend. The possibility of that friendship occurring is pretty remote if you do not introduce yourself, spend some time with them, observe who they are or what they have done, and share some of your thoughts and concerns about life with them. Our spiritual health is often strengthened or weakened by the choices we make through this spirit component within us.

We have all witnessed choices that we or others have made that have led to a lot of heartache. Choices that occur on the spur of the moment can be very tempting at times but also very dangerous. Life is "riddled with evils, mysteries, and troubles beyond human grasping and fixing."[13] No matter what kind of life we have built or set into motion, illness, loss of family members, job disappointments, and conflicts frequently happen. When they do, a process of understanding and discernment is needed in order to maintain our spiritual, physical, mental, and emotional health. These only develop as we exercise our spirit through reflection and processing of the things around us as well as requesting wisdom from God.

I would like to again summarize how the spirit (or heart) functions to allow us to make choices. As the human body receives input from the eyes or one of our other senses, the brain receives that input. Thoughts and ideas form in the brain. From those thoughts and ideas, the human spirit formulates choices and decisions based on the processing of that input. The brain is not programmed to independently produce a choice just based on input. There is nothing robotic about the human being. The human operates by choices made from the input it receives. Our final decision or choice depends on how our spirit has been shaped. That is the relationship-building part of the spirit that requires frequent connection of our spirit with the Creator in order to make better decisions for which we were designed. I became a better little league baseball player on the mound and at the plate because I engaged in and practiced those principles and skills that others who knew the game (and sometimes knew the thoughts of the creator of the game) much better than I, suggested I practice. The same principle applies to strengthening our spirit by the practice of engaging God's Spirit through prayer, the Word, meditation, and listening in order to discern and better understand the world around us.

What began for me in medical school as this great interest in science and how the human body functions morphed into an insatiable appetite and desire for learning more about these "unseen" aspects of the human being. The amazing complexity and the amazing consistency of the human body cannot be denied because of the millions of pages of reproducible data collected by millions of different medical people on numerous continents. I think as you allow time for the information to sink in that was presented about the spirit and how decisions and choices are made; it will allow you to see how the body operates in its totality. I hope that if you did not believe in God's existence before, were unsure, or just needed more evidence to have a stronger belief, this book has been informative in some way. The decision to believe or not believe in the existence of God only comes about by acquiring information through some format and sorting through the information in order to draw a conclusion. I believe that decision has eternal consequences. With this book, I hope that you have been able to see with your own eyes and other senses additional information that you may not have considered in the past. I believe there is plenty of information available by simply visualizing and sensing the things in nature that are right before us—especially the human body.

Last Thoughts

Instead of giving you four facts at the beginning of this chapter, I would like to leave you with four questions to ponder. Also, consider Appendix A for further thoughts about the human heart (spirit).

1. If not God, then who or what created the human body with its complexity and consistency?
2. If there was no creation and everything originated from matter, as some theories suggest, where did matter originate?
3. If we evolved from lesser beings, where is the evidence that points to those evolutionary forms that should exist in transition at this time?
4. In making a decision about the existence of God, what is at risk if we get it wrong?

APPENDIX A

BIBLICAL REFERENCES TO THE HEART (SPIRIT, WILL, CHOICE)

I previously mentioned that the Bible refers to the heart some 725 times in the RSV. All but a few of those times, it refers to this deep inner core of decision making and reasoning. Here are a few examples of the heart (spirit, will, choice) that are found in the Bible:

- Ecclesiastes 3:11: "He has made everything beautiful in its time. He has also set eternity in the human *heart*." There is an eternal component to our spirit that is engaged in life lived with God *now* as well as in our afterlife.
- Proverbs 4:23: "Above all else, guard your *heart*, for everything you do flows from it." Our thoughts, feelings, and ideas are processed through or within our human spirit.
- Proverbs 14:30: "A *heart* at peace gives life to the body, but envy rots the bones." Bones here likely refers to the human body in totality as the bones are the deep, main structural support of the body. There is nothing much better for the body, as a whole, than peace.

- Psalm 26:2: "Test me Lord and try me, examine my *heart* and my mind." This reveals that there is a difference between the mind (brain) and the heart (spirit).
- Proverbs 20:27: "The human *spirit* is the lamp of the Lord that sheds light on one's inmost being."
- Proverbs 27:19: "As water reflects the face, one's life reflects the *heart*." Before there were mirrors, water was a way to get a reflection as to what your appearance was. Similarly, one's life and face reflect the heart or spirit of who you are internally as an individual.
- Proverbs 3:5: "Trust in the Lord with all your *heart*. Don't lean on your own understanding." Remember the human's owner's manual, the Bible.
- Ecclesiastes 12:7: "And the dust returns to the ground it came from, and the *spirit* returns to God who gave it." The God-given spirit separates from the body and returns to him.
- Zechariah 12:1: "A prophecy: The word of the Lord…who forms the human *spirit* within a person."
- Matthew 5:8: "Blessed are the pure in *heart*, for they will see God." God is found in those whose hearts are in unison with his.
- Matthew 13:15: "For this people's *heart* has become calloused." Having the wrong thoughts and ideas, harboring anger and envy leads to calloused, poorly functioning spirits.
- Matthew 15:18: "Out of the *heart* comes evil thoughts." Depending on how we process our thoughts and ideas within our core being (spirit) will depend on how the thoughts are formed and put into action.
- Matthew 6:21: "For where your treasure is, there your *heart* will be also." Where you spend your time and the things that you cherish the most reflect what you consider to be the most important food to feed your spirit.

- Matthew 27:50: "And when Jesus had cried out again in a loud voice, he gave up his *spirit.*" At death, our earthly body separates from our spirit—even in the case of Jesus.

Notes

1. NC Science Now. How many daily decisions do we make? 2018.
2. Albert Camus, "The Wind of Djemila" in Albert Camus, ed. Harold Bloom, Bloom's BioCritiques (Philadelphia: Chelsea House, 2003), 59.
3. Revelation 21:1–2, Revised Standard Version (RSV), Tecarta Bible App.
4. Hebrews 11:1 RSV.
5. Romans 1:20 RSV.
6. Dictionary.com.
7. Michael J. Behe, Darwin's Black Box: The Biochemical Challenge to Evolution (1996, 2006), preface, x.
8. N. T. Wright, Matthew for Everyone, Part 1 (2004), 63.
9. Dallas Willard, Renovation of the Heart (2002), 29–30.
10. N. T. Wright, Paul, the Pastoral Letters for Everyone (2004); 2 Timothy 3:16, p. 121.
11. Tim Keller with Kathy Keller, God's Wisdom for Navigating Life (2017), 67.
12. Peter Scazzero, Emotionally Healthy Spirituality (2017), 117.
13. Raymond C. Van Leeuwen, "Book of Proverbs," in The New Interpreter's Bible, vol. 5 (Nashville: Abingdon, 1997), 50.

ABOUT THE AUTHOR

Troy Vines, M.D. is a husband, father, grandfather, family physician, and church elder. He lives in Jonesboro, Arkansas, where he currently practices medicine. He is an elder at Compass Church in Jonesboro. He is an alumnus of Arkansas State University and later received his pharmacy degree, became a registered pharmacist (RPh), followed by a doctor of medicine degree (MD) both from the University of Arkansas for Medical Sciences in Little Rock, Arkansas.

Printed in the USA
CPSIA information can be obtained
at www.ICGtesting.com
LVHW022235090524
779584LV00004B/416

9 781685 700294